FAIRFAX COUNTY

Historical Highlights

From 1607

by

Jean Geddes

©1967, DENLINGER'S
LIBRARY OF CONGRESS CATALOG CARD NUMBER: 67-16331

Published By
DENLINGER'S
Fairfax, Virginia 22030

FOREWORD

Fairfax County, Virginia, has been described as one of the most distinguished counties in the entire Nation. It is, indeed, for the history of this county is, in miniature, the history of Virginia and may be regarded as typical of the Colonial period of our country.

Although the first families who built their houses in the area were mainly English, it shortly became the new home of Scotch, Irish, German, Swiss and others who were escaping from the economic turmoil taking place in Europe. The area soon became a part of the great melting pot which was to make up America.

In its various stages of growth, the county experienced rapid agricultural development, produced active and prosperous urban centers and realized periods of productive commerce and shipping. The political life influenced the development of the Colonies and Fairfax claims two of the Nation's greatest citizens: George Washington, first President of the country and George Mason, author of the Virginia Declaration of Rights.

The magnificent scenic beauty of the county from the Great Falls of the Potomac to the rolling, fertile farmlands has been the subject for many an artist's canvas.

Some of the most historic homes in Virginia, such as Mount Vernon, Gunston Hall, Woodlawn, Sully and many others, are in this county. At the time of their construction, three historic churches: The Falls Church, Pohick Church, and Christ Church in Alexandria, were all in Fairfax County.

Today, the county is the adopted home of families from various parts of the Nation and the world. It is the purpose of this book to acquaint all, new residents as well as old, with the rich heritage of the county as well as with the bright promise of its future, so that they may take a just pride in their home, Fairfax County, Virginia.

Fairfax Courthouse

ACKNOWLEDGMENTS

The preparation of such a book as this would have been quite impossible were it not for the help of many persons who took both the time and trouble to answer many questions and in some cases to probe into their family papers in order to find accurate dates and data.

In grateful and sincere appreciation I would like to list their names:

Mr. A. Smith Bowman	Miss Elsie Mathews
Mr. C.J.S. Durham	Mr. and Mrs. Harry Middleton
Mr. Charles Gage	Miss Rebecca Middleton
Mrs. Edward Howrey	Mr. and Mrs. Lyle Millan
Mr. Virgil Carrington Jones	Mrs. Charles Pozer
Mr. James Keith	Mrs. Jeanne Rust
Mrs. Bernice Lionsdale	Mrs. Katherine Snyder Shands
Mr. R.M. Loughborough	Mrs. Eleanor Lee Templeman
Mr. Donald McAfee	Mr. Edward Wagstaff
Mr. Carlton Massey	Mrs. Ruth Williams

Mr. and Mrs. Charles Bretschneider
John W. McDonald, Col., U.S. Army (Ret.)

The following groups of people:

Arlington County Historical Society	Falls Church Library Staff
Fairfax County Historical Society	Fairfax County Library Staff
Fairfax County Administrative Offices	Mt. Vernon Ladies Association
Fairfax County Information Centers	Woodlawn Plantation
Arlington County Library Staff	

Administrative offices of Pohick Church and the Falls Church Episcopal Church for providing literature regarding the buildings.

For the photographs in the book I wish to thank:

Mr. Charles Baptie	Mrs. Virginia Ludwig
Judge Paul Brown	Mr. Robert Owens
Mr. Tom Chapman	Mr. Ray Shaffner
Mrs. Virginia Copeland	The Library of Congress
Mr. Wilmer Holbrook	The National Archives
Mr. Lee Hubbard	The Northern Virginia Sun Newspaper
Mr. A. Frank Krause	The Vienna Virginian

For careful reading of the manuscript and valuable critical suggestions I am most grateful to:

Mr. William W. Denlinger   Mrs. R. Annabel Rathman

TABLE OF CONTENTS

Exploration of "The Northern Neck"	7
Early Government in Fairfax County	12
Early Laws	15
"Ordinaries"	17
Early Roads	19
Chain Bridge	24
Early Railroads	27
Life on the Great Plantations	33
Religious Life in the Early Days of the County	39
Thomas, Sixth Lord Fairfax	45
The Code Duello	47
George Washington of Mt. Vernon Plantation	49
George Mason of Gunston Hall	51
"King" Carter's Copper Mine	55
George Washington's Potowmack Canal Project	59
Matildaville	63
Woodlawn Plantation	65
Sully	69
Ravensworth, Ossian Hall and Oak Hill	75
Oakley	81
The James Wren House	82
Fairfax County and the Civil War	83
Captain James W. Jackson and Colonel Elmer E. Ellsworth	87
Mosby's Capture of General Stoughton	91
The Burke Station Raid	98
J.E.B. Stuart at His Camp	101
Professor Lowe and His Balloon	103
Clara Barton, Heroine of the Second Battle of Manassas	105
The Rebel Yell	109
Antonia Ford of Fairfax	111
Towns and Settlements in Fairfax County	114
Historic Facts	126
Fairfax County Today	128

Display at Museum of Arlington Historical Society shows model Indian village typical of seventeenth century tribes living in Northern Neck area.

Exploration of "The Northern Neck"

Captain John Smith is the first European known positively to have explored the area which today constitutes Northern Virginia. It is believed that the Spanish may have explored the Potomac River earlier, but no records of their explorations have ever been found.

Smith had been sent out from the Jamestown Colony by the Virginia Company, which was seeking gold as well as a Northwest passage to the Pacific, and he and his party explored more than three thousand miles of coastline -- ocean and rivers -- during 1607, 1608, and 1609, going up the Potomac by boat in 1608 as far as the little falls. The men endured great hardships during the journey and were constantly under attack from the Indians of the Powhatan Confederacy, who shot at them with arrows and attempted to lure them into ambushes on the land. Near the falls line, Smith's party encountered Indians that were friendly. These were the Piscataways, Anacostans and Tauxenents, who were then attempting to break with the Powhatan Confederacy and become allied with the Iroquois.

No gold was found by the explorers, other than an inferior grade of ore which the Indians used as body paint. Nor was a Northwest passage found. What Smith and his party did find was a land of majestic beauty and tremendous natural resources, bountifully populated with game -- deer, buffalo, geese, ducks, turkeys, and fish. In fact, the fish in the river were so abundant that, lacking nets, Smith's companions scooped them up with their frying pans.

In the party accompanying Smith was Captain Powell, who, together with Smith, is credited with having drawn the first maps of the area. Smith himself made a detailed record of the explorations along the river and when he returned to Jamestown he told of the awesome spectacle of the falls where the waters of the Potomac were hurled down seventy-five feet over the great rocks in the river below, making navigation through the area impossible. He described the magnificent trees from which the Indians fashioned their canoes. And he tried to convince the settlers of Jamestown that they should adopt the Indians' methods of sustaining themselves -- clearing the underbrush to provide land on which to cultivate corn, tobacco, and potatoes, and encouraging the pasturing of deer and buffalo nearby, so as to provide a ready supply of food for the winter months. It is unfortunate indeed that Smith's advice was not needed. As the histories of early Virginia so vividly tell, much of the tragedy of those first winters would have been avoided had the settlers adopted the Indians' ways.

Following Smith's journeys, a number of years passed before any settlement was established along the Potomac, though other parties explored the area. Among them was a group led by a young English nobleman, Henry Spelman, who also journeyed upstream as far as the falls.

Henry Fleet, who had accompanied Spelman on this journey, was taken captive by the Indians and held for several years. Later he was freed but continued to live in the area and developed a lucrative business trading with the tribes. It was so lucrative, in fact, that he acquired three ships in which to transport his wares -- the beads, knives, and cloth that he imported and traded for the furs he shipped back to England.

Fleet, describing this land that later became Fairfax County, said, "This place without question is the most pleasant and healthful in all the country and most convenient for habitation. The air temperate in summer and not violent in winter. It aboundeth in all manner of fish, and as for deer, buffalo, bear, turkey, the woods do swarm with them, and the soil is exceedingly fertile."

Still another explorer was Captain Samuel Argall, who explored the area in 1613, and who is said to have kidnapped the lovely Pocahontas from the Indians at the mouth of Potomac Creek. It was while she was being held captive among the English that Pocahontas met and later married John Rolfe.

Although a great influx of settlers did not take place immediately, the enthusiastic reports of returning explorers encouraged residents at the mouth of the Chesapeake to move on up the Bay's western shore to lay claim to the land, construct small houses and push deeper into the hills. The Indians, in turn, were slowly pushed back.

The life of the early settler was a rigorous one, however, for there was constant danger of attack by unfriendly Indians. The only source of organized protection lay in the Potomac Rangers, who patrolled the Northern Virginia area until 1722, when Governor Spottswood drew up a treaty with the Iroquois Nation, confining the tribes beyond the Blue Ridge. Under the terms of the treaty, Virginia was given title to "all lands within the said Colony as it is now or hereafter may be peopled and bounded."

The region that Sir Walter Raleigh named "Virginia" in honor of the Virgin Queen, Elizabeth, covered the entire east coast of the continent from what is now New England south to Florida. But as various commercial groups arrived on the new continent -- first to exploit the land and the natives in search of gold and silver, later to colonize -- segments of the original tract were renamed. By the time the Thirteen Colonies had been established, the area known as Virginia had shrunk to encompass only what is now Virginia and West Virginia.

Since most of the settlers were English and the Virginia Colony was originally under British rule, the governmental jurisdictions were modeled on those of England. Thus, the various settlements which had been made in the Colony were, by an act of the General Assembly passed in 1634, organized into several counties: the Isle of Wight (west of the James River), Henrico, Warwick, Elizabeth City, James City, and Charles City (between the James and the Rappahannock Rivers), and Northampton (on the Eastern Shore of the Chesapeake Bay). In 1648, the isolated settlements made at Chicoen, on the lower Potomac, were organized into another county, Northumberland.

The remaining area, that which lay between the Potomac and Rappahannock Rivers and extended from the Chesapeake Bay to the headwaters of the rivers high in the Allegheny Mountains, was known as the "Northern Neck of Virginia."

In 1649, King Charles II of England gave to seven English noblemen friends, the five million acres comprising this entire area of the Northern Neck Proprietary (later known as the Fairfax Proprietary). The new owners of the land were permitted to dispose of areas not already appropriated by settlers, to make grants to new settlers, and to collect rents and fees.

Eventually, the entire tract was acquired by Thomas, Lord Culpeper, one of the original seven. It was inherited from him by his widow, Margaret, who, upon her death in 1710, left it to her widowed daughter, Catherine, Lady Fairfax. Since she continued to reside in England, Lady Catherine entrusted the management of her Colonial interests to Thomas Corbin, a London merchant who did business in Virginia. It was at Corbin's suggestion that Lady Catherine leased the Proprietary to Edmund Jennings. Jennings resided in England, too, so Thomas Lee acted for him and was in sole charge of the management of the Proprietary for several years.

Upon the death of Lady Fairfax, the Proprietary was inherited by her son Thomas, Sixth Lord Fairfax, who later became one of the most colorful figures in Colonial Virginia. Lord Fairfax resided in England at the time he inherited the Proprietary, and he first visited Virginia in 1736. He was so impressed with the Colony that upon his return to England the following year, he began to dispose of his English and Scottish holdings and prepared to return to the new land. This he finally did in 1747, and he remained in Virginia for the rest of his life.

Colonization had advanced rapidly during the century that elapsed between the time the Northern Neck passed into the possession of Lord Culpeper and the time when Charles, Lord Fairfax, established his home there. In 1653, the County of Westmoreland had been organized in the southernmost portion of the Proprietary. Then in 1663, Stafford County was organized; in 1730, Prince William; and in 1742, the remaining portion of the Northern Neck became Fairfax County. Extending from the Potomac and Occoquan Rivers to the Blue Ridge Mountains, it included the present area known as Fairfax County, as well as the Counties of Loudoun and Arlington, and the Cities of Alexandria, Fairfax, and Falls Church.

The original Fairfax County did not exist long, for in 1757, the Virginia House of Burgesses passed an Act cutting off from it the County of Loudoun. The dividing line between the two counties stood for forty-one years, and then in 1798, the General Assembly of Virginia passed an Act that provided a new dividing line -- one which has remained to the present day as the boundary between Fairfax and Loudoun Counties.

In the meantime, the Revolution had been fought and won, and the Thirteen Colonies had become the United States of America. Article I, Section 8, of the Constitution of the United States, empowered Congress

Great Falls of the Potomac

High water at Great Falls reveals the enormous burden of the Potomac's 11,000-square-mile drainage basin.

to accept a territory not to exceed ten miles square, to be set aside as the permanent seat of the Federal Government. In 1789, the Virginia Legislature had offered to cede such a tract, or to join with Maryland and Pennsylvania in ceding an area. Thus, the District of Columbia was eventually laid off on lands that were to be ceded by Maryland and Virginia. The portion to be ceded by Virginia began at Jones Point at the mouth of Great Hunting Creek and encompassed the Town of Alexandria and a portion of the County of Fairfax along the western bank of the Potomac.

The cornerstone for the District of Columbia was set at Jones Point on April 15, 1791, and the area to be ceded then became known as the County of Alexandria. Congress and the Government offices were removed from Philadelphia to the City of Washington in 1800, and Federal jurisdiction was extended over the County of Alexandria early in 1801.

But dissatisfaction arose among the inhabitants of Alexandria County, for they did not relish being a part of the District of Columbia. So in 1846, the Virginia General Assembly adopted an Act expressing the willingness of Virginia to accept the return of the territory, should the Federal Government agree to re-cede it. An Act of Congress followed, authorizing the President of the United States to transfer back that part of the District of Columbia that lay on the Virginia side of the Potomac, should the inhabitants approve. They approved very much, so on September 7, 1846, the retrocession was put into effect. In March of the following year the Virginia General Assembly extended the Commonwealth's jurisdiction over the County of Alexandria and provided that it should be a separate county and retain the name of "Alexandria." Thus, what is now Arlington County was at that time a part of Alexandria County and remained so until the 1920's, when it became a county in its own right.

Stone marking the 1746 western boundary of the estate of Lord Fairfax was found near Ingham, Virginia, on line between properties of Frank Hilliard and Virgil Dovel and is to be on permanent display at Big Meadows visitors' center in Shenandoah National Park. Shown in photo with marker is Frank Hilliard's grandson.

Early Government in Fairfax County

The Virginia General Assembly is the oldest legislative body on the North American Continent and was organized long before the Revolutionary War was fought and the United States came into being. Under authority granted by the King of England, the first General Assembly of Virginia was organized by Sir George Yeardly, with himself as governor, a six member council appointed by him, and a twenty-two member House of Burgesses elected by the freemen in the eleven plantations -- as the eleven legislative districts were called. This first legislative body in America convened for the first time on July 30, 1619, and, although changes gradually took place in its proceedings and in the authority of the body, the Virginia General Assembly remained responsible for the administration of all Virginia affairs throughout the Colonial period.

As mentioned previously, governmental jurisdictions in the Colony had evolved along the same lines as those of legislative bodies then extant in England. Thus, as the population of the Colony increased and it became necessary to make new laws and provide means to administer them, the Virginia Assembly created counties, and in each county set up a county court. Until about the middle of the nineteenth century, responsibility for administrative as well as judicial functions was completely centered in the county courts, so the history of any Virginia county was reflected in its court records. Just as the town meeting provided the basis of the government in New England, so the county court constituted the concept of government that prevailed in Colonial Virginia.

The county courts not only maintained order and sat in judgment in all cases of law or chancery (other than those involving "outlawry") but also supervised elections; appointed county officials; directed the administration of estates and supervised the care of indigents and orphans; levied taxes; paid bills and settled claims against the county; directed construction of public buildings and roads; licensed taverns, ordinaries, and warehouses; and appointed inspectors of tar, turpentine, tobacco, flour, pork, and beef.

In addition to being directly responsible for the appointment of minor county officials, the justices of the county courts were indirectly responsible for appointment of more important county officials, for it was upon the recommendations of the courts that the governor commissioned the sheriff, the coroner, and the county militia officers.

The justices themselves were appointed for life by the governor. When a vacancy occurred as the result of the death of an incumbent, the governor appointed a successor on the basis of the recommendations of the remaining justices. Thus, there may have been some grounds for the charge that the courts represented a self-perpetuating hierarchy.

Individual justices were responsible for maintaining order in their own jurisdictions, handling suits for small debts, issuing peace bonds, and ordering those accused of serious offenses to appear before regular court sessions, where the justices met to act as a body in all other cases except those involving "life and limb." Appeals to the General Court in Williamsburg were permitted in criminal cases and in civil cases involving more than five pounds sterling. From the decisions of the General Court, a citizen could appeal to the Crown, though such appeals apparently were made but infrequently.

Because the justices were unable to maintain order over extremely large areas, the General Assembly divided counties into parishes and within each parish, appointed vestrymen with civil authority. Actually, parishes were created throughout the Northern Neck Proprietary before all of the counties were organized. Therefore, certain parishes in the Northern Neck have existed for a longer period of time than have the counties in which they are now located. For example, the Parish of Truro was established before there was a County of Fairfax. In fact, when the county was established, its boundaries were the same as those previously established for the Parish of Truro.

Once the Parish of Truro had been created, an effort was made by the citizens of the parish to bring about the organization of a county with its own court, which would be apart from Prince William -- the county which then had jurisdiction over Truro and hence over the area which was to become Fairfax County. William Fairfax, cousin of the Lord Proprietor, Thomas Fairfax, ran for the office of Burgess in the Assembly, and upon his election, he was charged by the voters to bring about the formation of the new county. This he did, introducing in the General Assembly the Act which resulted in the establishment of Fairfax County in 1742.

The Act provided that a court for the new County of Fairfax should be held by the justices of the county upon the third Thursday in every month "in such manner as by the laws of this colony is provided, and shall be by their commissions directed." The court thus established as the governing body of Fairfax County was maintained as directed from 1742 until 1902, when, through revision of the Virginia Constitution, it was superseded by a new form of county government.

The first Fairfax court session was probably held on the north side of the Occoquan River and may have been held in the building used by its predecessor, the Prince William County court.

In 1743 the county seat was established in the area called "Spring Field," which included the present Freedom Hill and Tyson's Corners areas. The name "Spring Field" presumably was derived from the fact that the area encompassed springs which were the sources of the Accotink, Wolf Trap, Pimmitt, and Scott Runs.

There is no trace today of this first courthouse, although it remained on the site for ten years. Then the citizens of Alexandria asked that the court be relocated within the boundaries of their town, and the General Assembly, responding to pressure from influential citizens, so ordered.

Although the new courthouse in Alexandria was not entirely completed until 1754, the court was transferred in April 1752 to a site at the intersection of Cameron and Fairfax Streets, next to the public market in Alexandria. By 1788 the building was in such a state of decay that repairs were needed badly. Virginia was now a Commonwealth of the United States and the General Assembly was considering the bill to cede the land for the District of Columbia to the Federal Government. So in view of the probability that the town of Alexandria would become a part of the District of Columbia, the General Assembly voted to move the Fairfax County Courthouse to its present site. The property on Little River Turnpike was purchased from Richard Ratcliffe and the present building was completed in 1800. The settlement that grew up around the courthouse was first known as Providence, but later the name was changed to Fairfax. One of the county's magisterial districts still retains the name of Providence, however.

Photo taken about 1928 of building then used as Fairfax County Clerk's office.

Early Laws

Under early Colonial laws, hog stealing was considered a most serious crime and one which justified severe punishment. The law stated that anyone convicted of stealing or unlawfully killing a hog belonging to another, must pay 1,000 pounds of tobacco to the owner of the hog and a like amount to the informer. If the convicted person was unable to pay the debt, he was then sentenced to two years of forced servitude -- one year in service to the owner and the other in service to the informer. In 1679 the law was expanded so that for a second offense a convicted thief was to be punished by being forced to stand two hours in the pillory, and, in addition, to lose his ears; for a third offense the suspect was to be tried by the laws of England as in the case of felony.

In 1662, a law was enacted which provided that any master of a ship bringing a Quaker to live in the Colony after July of that year would be fined "5,000 pounds of tobacco, to be levied by distress and sale of his goods and enjoined to carry him, her, or them, out of the county again."

In 1755, the year of the Braddock War, the General Assembly passed a law that provided for the payment of ten pounds for every Indian enemy above the age of twelve taken prisoner or killed within the Colony during the space of two years following adjournment of the Assembly.

The General Assembly required that each court set up near the courthouse a pillory, stocks, whipping post, and ducking stool. The latter was a device brought over from England and was used primarily as a means for punishing scolding women, the philosophy apparently being that water would quench the heat of an angry tongue.

Each county court was also required to set up a gallows. The Fairfax County court set up its gallows at Freedom Hill when the courthouse was built at Spring Field, and the gallows remained at Freedom Hill when the court was moved to Alexandria. According to local historians, Gallows Road derived its name from the fact that offenders tried in the court in Alexandria and sentenced to be hanged, were transported by way of the Little River Turnpike to Gallows Road and thence to the gallows at Freedom Hill.

According to early court records, the laws most frequently violated were those dealing with the sale of intoxicating liquors without a license, drunkenness, assault and battery, disorderly conduct, trespassing, and use of profane language. These offenses, as well as those resulting from moral laxity, were punishable by fine, by whipping, or by imprisonment in the county jail. But often offenders were also subjected to the public disgrace of spending time in the stocks and the pillory or of being "ducked." In such cases, the offender was shamed additionally by having attached to his person during the period of punishment, a large placard on which was printed the nature of the offense, so that all who saw him should know.

Because tobacco was for many years the main source of income and during Colonial times was a standard medium of exchange, fines and court charges were levied in tobacco. For whipping a person, the sheriff was paid twenty pounds of tobacco; for placing an offender in the stocks, ten pounds; for pillorying a person, twenty pounds; for ducking a scolding woman, twenty pounds; for hanging a felon, two hundred and fifty pounds; for probating a will, fifty pounds; and for issuing a marriage license, twenty pounds.

Slave market, Alexandria, Virginia

"Ordinaries"

Taverns and inns in Colonial days were usually called "ordinaries," and as has been mentioned before, the keepers of ordinaries were licensed by the courts, which also established rates for the meals and accommodations provided. Included in the early price-control laws were "liquors, diet, lodging, provender, stableage, fodder and pasturage." The court order establishing prices also enjoined the innkeeper to place the price list near the door and not higher than six feet from the floor. Not only were the cost and quantity of the food regulated by law, but also the quality, for food was ordered to be wholesome as well as plentiful.

Until 1639, six pounds of tobacco was the standard charge for a dinner. Through the years prices varied somewhat. They were never low, although they were reduced when food became unusually plentiful. During one period of fluctuating prices, the exorbitant price of twenty pounds of tobacco was charged for a master's meal and fifteen pounds was charged for a servant's meal. High prices were due in part to the fact that innkeepers had few guests, but also were due to the fact that tobacco leaf varied in quality and the innkeeper always faced the risk that the tobacco might depreciate in value before he had an opportunity to market it.

In 1757, the price for a hot diet was quoted as nine pence, and for a cold diet, six pence. A traveler at that time who still preferred to carry his fortune in the form of tobacco, presumably could pay his bill with an appropriate number of pounds of leaf.

Since the ordinaries were centers for the exchange of news and other important information of the day, the keeper of an ordinary was regarded much as is the editor of a newspaper today. In addition to news passed on by word of mouth, the ordinary provided much information on public taxes, runaway servants, stolen horses, etc., for handbills containing such data were usually plastered in a prominent place.

Colonial ordinaries were much alike in outward appearance. Most of them were frame buildings with a porch across the front. Guests usually slept in a common room, often on mattresses laid on the floor. Meals were served at a designated hour with guests grouped around a common table and the innkeeper serving as host.

Often, planters who were lonely for company would send a servant to the tavern to invite guests to visit in their homes. For relinquishing his guests, the keeper was compensated by gifts from the planter.

Of the many inns in Fairfax County, one of the more prominent was Earp's Ordinary, owned by the Earp family, which came to Virginia from Maryland and established the ordinary before 1742.

Earp's Ordinary became such a popular place that at one time the area immediately surrounding it was known as Earp's Corner. When the Little River Turnpike was paved, tolls were collected at the inn.

Earp's Ordinary is still standing at 10386 East Main Street in the City of Fairfax. An attractive pink brick dwelling, it is now the private residence of Mrs. Charles Pozer.

Earp's Ordinary

Early Roads

The inland roads of Virginia began as buffalo trails leading from the pastures in the lowlands, going on over the Blue Ridge and into the valleys beyond. Because the buffalo literally followed the path of least resistance, they picked their way judiciously over the rough terrain, avoiding steep inclines and rocky outcroppings. Thus, the buffalo trails actually constituted the most practical routes over the hills. The Indians followed the buffalo paths, as did the explorers and fur traders later on. And even today, many of Virginia's heavily traveled roads follow much the same paths as did those buffalo trails of yesterday.

Throughout the Colonies the roads were poor, so the Virginia roads were probably typical of the times. But anyone making a lengthy trip employed a guide, for travelers in the Colony could easily become lost, even in broad daylight, on the narrow, poorly marked trails. Most of the cross-country traveling was done on horseback, with carriages being used only to attend church or to make short trips to visit with friends.

The early settlements and the plantation homes were usually built close to the river banks, so much of the traveling in the Colony was done by barge or boat. Nevertheless, several important roads in Fairfax County came into being during Colonial times. The oldest was the Potomac Path, which ran between Alexandria and Fredericksburg and is now U.S. Route 1 to the south. This road developed as a highway partly through the progress of land settlement but more directly as the result of the 1662 Road Act of the Virginia Assembly, which required every county to "appoint surveyors of highways who shall lay out the most convenient wayes to Church, to the Court, to Jamestown and from county to county." Thus, along the main roads in Colonial times were to be found the churches, chapels, and courthouses, though many were later removed to other locations.

What became the Little River Turnpike, leading from Alexandria to the west, was another important early road. Freight from as far away as the Ohio Valley was hauled over this route to the busy seaport of Belhaven -- as Alexandria was called when it was established as a townsite in 1745.

In 1785, heavy traffic had caused the original roadbed to deteriorate to such an extent that it was necessary to build a new one, "an artificial bed of pounded or broken stone." In 1795, the Virginia Legislature chartered the turnpike, the first in the United States, as the Little River Turnpike Company. Finished in 1811, the road was thirty-four miles long, with wooden bridges across the numerous streams along the route. The wooden bridges were soon replaced by stone arches, some of which are still in use today.

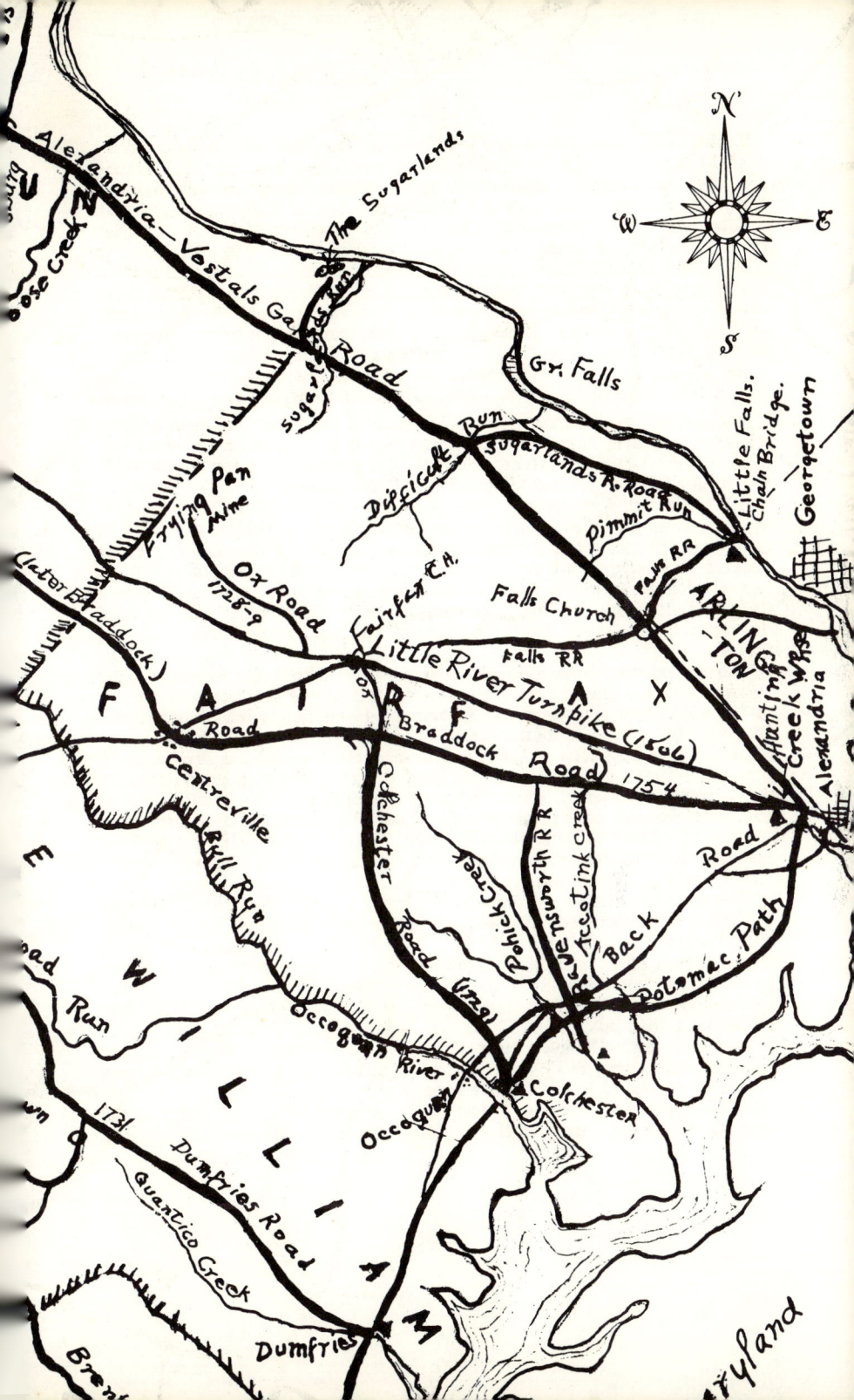

Tolls were collected on the Little River Turnpike until 1896, when the road became a part of the State's network of highways. Although the road has been rebuilt and widened, some of the crushed stone from the original turnpike remains even now as part of the fill for the present roadbed.

Little River Turnpike parallels the old Braddock Road, which today is of local significance only. When the connection was established in 1754, however, the road was expected to be the one General Braddock would use on his march against the French and Indians. Historians are not in complete agreement as to the route he actually took, but a majority feel he did not choose Braddock Road, but instead sent part of his army through Maryland and the rest over the Eastern Ridge Road through Falls Church, the Leesburg area, and Charles Town. Nevertheless, the road which he evidently never used, still bears General Braddock's name.

Eastern Ridge Road, now Route 7, is one of the oldest and most heavily traveled roads in Northern Virginia. Originally it terminated at an inn, or ordinary, where the Hunting Creek Warehouse was later established. It now leads from Alexandria, through Falls Church, and on to Leesburg and Winchester. Part of the route was laid out in 1699 by a mission sent by the governor of Virginia to the emperor of the Piscataway tribe on Conoy Island near the present Point of Rocks. As the road came into general use, it was known by various names: New Church Road, for the new church from which the town of Falls Church took its name; Eastern Ridge Road; Vestal's Gap Road; Middle Pike; and eventually that part of the road which is in the city of Falls Church became known as Broad Street.

The Sugarlands Rolling Road led from the Little Falls crossing of the Potomac northwestward to Difficult Run, then up the south side of the run to a ford, north to a point apparently in the neighborhood of present Dranesville, and east to the Sugarland holdings of Daniel McCarty. The Sugarlands was an area of sugar maples near the Potomac, at the boundary between Fairfax and Loudoun Counties, discovered by rangers on Indian duty. Daniel McCarty, who was from Westmoreland County and was at one time Speaker of the House in the General Assembly, took out the first patent (or claim) on land above Great Falls. His Sugarlands Rolling Road is now the Old Georgetown-Leesburg Turnpike from Chain Bridge to Great Falls and Dranesville.

The term "rolling" was derived from the fact that the great hogsheads of tobacco transported to the warehouses and shipping centers, were rolled over the roads. A wooden pin was driven into each head of the cask, then rude shafts were attached to the two pins so that the hogshead looked somewhat like the garden roller of the present day. With motive power furnished by men, oxen, or horses, the hogshead was then rolled to its destination.

Some of the tollhouses built along the various turnpikes remained in use until the early 1900's. Falls Church had two tollhouses located along Route 7, and one is known to have been in use as late as 1912.

A tollhouse still stands a few yards off Route 7 at Broad Run on the way to Leesburg, about eighteen miles from the city of Falls Church.

When it was first constructed, the building consisted of one large room, an attic, and a basement. It was large enough to house only the tollkeeper, who collected the fees from travelers coming from the mountains beyond Leesburg on their way to Alexandria. Now a private home, the central part of the house has been restored to its original state. A wing has been added on either side of the original structure, and a patio and swimming pool have been built at the rear of the building. Two large stone pillars in the front of the property support a handsome, wrought iron gate, showing where the original driveway was located.

To the east of the tollhouse is an old stone bridge, no longer in use but standing today as a monument to a bygone era. Construction of the bridge is credited to Claude Crozet, well-known soldier who served as Virginia State Engineer about 1832. He is also credited with having planned a great development of inland communication (road, canal, and railroad) which, although not completed in its entirety, eventually made Virginia's transportation system one of the best in the country.

Tollhouse at Broad Run

Chain Bridge

The first bridge constructed at the site of the present Chain Bridge was a covered timber structure designed by Timothy Palmer and built in 1797 by the Georgetown Potomac Bridge Company, which issued 400 shares of stock with a value of $200 each. Originally an Indian crossing, the location was chosen because the river was narrow enough in that particular area to make bridging relatively inexpensive.

The chief traffic over the bridge was the herds of cattle that were driven across from Fairfax County to the Georgetown auction markets. The herds were watered at Pimmit Run before crossing the bridge and after only seven years of use by this "watered stock" the bridge collapsed in 1804.

The second bridge built at the site was a suspension bridge completed in 1808 and known as the Chain Bridge. The roadway was 136 feet long and was suspended from huge chains anchored in stone abutments. But after only two years of use, flood waters swept the bridge away in 1810.

An Act of Congress in 1811 permitted the Georgetown Potomac Company to assess its stockholders for funds with which to rebuild the bridge. This third structure lasted until 1852, although private ownership ended in 1833. Bitter complaints had been raised over the high toll charges -- which included a fee of twenty-five cents for a horse -- and as a result, Congress appropriated $150,000 to permit the Georgetown Board of Aldermen and the Common Council to purchase and operate the bridge as a municipal activity. The toll charges were then abolished.

The bridge was seriously damaged in 1852 and the following year Congress appropriated money for its restoration.

The bridge played an important role during the Civil War as the connection between Federal troops in Fairfax County and the reserve encampments at Tennellytown on the District side. At that time, the bridge was of timbered truss construction on masonry piers. This type of construction is expected to have a lifespan of two hundred years, and some of the piers are still in place and still in use today.

In 1874, a new bridge was constructed, with eight iron trusses which were 1,350 feet long, overall. The bridge had a timber floor laid on the old stone abutments and was designed to carry a six-ton load. When the bridge was completed, the Reverend Mutersbaugh of Fairfax, a minister-farmer, was asked to make a test of the strength of the bridge. In a six-horse wagon loaded with wood, he drove across to Georgetown, where he deposited the wood and reloaded the wagon with fertilizer and drove back across the bridge. At the end of the trip, he declared that the bridge could support any load it would be called upon to carry.

The bridge remained in good useable condition until the 1920's, when it began to show the effects of the pounding flood waters and the ice jams. In 1926, serious signs of failure appeared, including a large cavity in the abutment on the Virginia side. Strict speed and load limits were designated by the District Commissioners in June 1927, and a twenty-four hour watch was instituted. During periods of high water, the bridge was closed to traffic. Considerable controversy arose, for the commuters using the bridge wanted it shut down only when real danger existed, while Arlington County officials wanted traffic stopped completely, since they feared damage might occur to the newly installed eight-inch water mains that ran under the structure and brought water to the county from the Dalecarlia Reservoir.

Finally, in July 1927, the bridge was closed so that repairs could be made to the Virginia side. A concrete pier was then built at a cost of $39,000.

The bridge reopened on August 11, 1928, during non-working hours only, so that repairs could continue. It went into full-time service later that month.

The flood of 1936 proved to be too much for the bridge, and in 1937 the superstructure was dismantled and the following year $393,000 was spent to build a steel cantilever girder structure, five feet higher from the river. This is the Chain Bridge that is in use today.

Chain Bridge (from the Brady Collection of the Library of Congress)

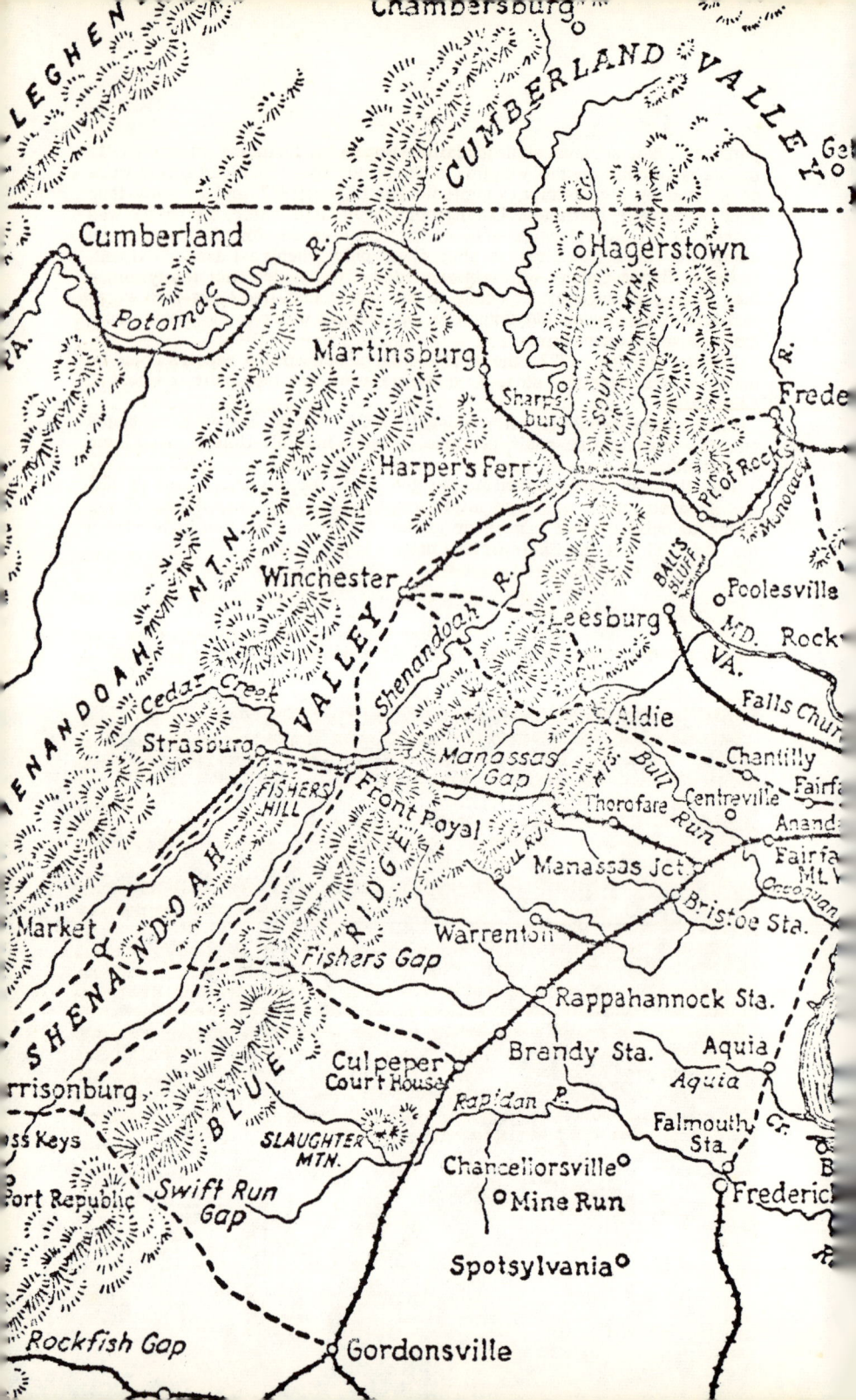

Early Railroads

The "Alexandria and Harpers Ferry Railroad" was chartered by the General Assembly on March 20, 1847, as an independent line which was to run from Alexandria to Harpers Ferry, where it was to join with the independent "Winchester and Potomac Railroad," thus establishing a direct line from the port of Alexandria to the West. However, in 1848, before construction had been started, the Baltimore and Ohio bought up the stock of the Winchester and Potomac, and plans for the Alexandria and Harpers Ferry line were dropped.

Six years later, the plans for a central railroad through Northern Virginia were revived, and a new company, under the name of "Alexandria, Loudoun and Hampshire Railroad," was organized on May 24, 1853. This time, the line was routed from Alexandria to Paddytown (now Keyser, West Virginia).

Grading was started in 1855, but money was scarce and it was not until 1858 that the tracks reached Leesburg, thirty-eight miles west of Alexandria. In 1859, the first wood-burning locomotives arrived and the road was in business.

When Virginia seceded from the Union at the outbreak of the Civil War, Union troops swarmed down on Alexandria from Washington and took over the railroads and docks. One of the line's four locomotives was captured at the outset, and other equipment was destroyed. As time went on, the tracks were damaged, and Federal troops confiscated the only remaining locomotive and burned most of the new freight and passenger cars. But throughout the war, the Union Army operated trains over the line from Alexandria west to Vienna.

At the close of the war, the rail property was given to the Virginia Board of Public Works and the original owners. As was the case with other railroads of the time, the Alexandria, Loudoun and Hampshire line was permitted to purchase equipment and rolling stock from the United States Military Railroads, under an agreement that permitted payments to be made from profits, once the line was again operational for commercial purposes.

Regular service was re-established in 1864 and the line prospered. Then it was renamed the "Washington and Ohio Railroad," and plans were made to extend the tracks 325 miles to Point Pleasant, West Virginia. Unfortunately, the line was not sufficiently prosperous to justify the hopeful plans of the owners, and the Washington and Ohio went into receivership. Sold for $400,000, it was reorganized as the "Washington and Western Railroad." But, again, financial problems plagued the company, and New York interests purchased the line, renaming it the "Washington, Ohio and Western." Converted first from steam to electric power, the line was later converted to diesel power.

In 1890, John R. McLean and Senator Stephen B. Elkins had established an electrically powered branch between Georgetown and Great Falls, which they named the "Great Falls and Old Dominion Railroad." When the trackage was extended further to the west in 1911, the name of the entire line was changed once again, this time to the name it bears today -- the "Washington and Old Dominion Railroad."

In March 1848, a group of Virginia planters petitioned the General Assembly for a charter for the "Orange and Alexandria Railroad Company," which was to run from Alexandria in a southwesterly direction across Fairfax County and on to Gordonsville. There, the line was to connect with the "Louisa Railroad" (later renamed the "Virginia Central Railroad," and still later, the "Chesapeake and Ohio Railroad"). The route proposed would thus provide a single trunk line connecting tidewater transportation facilities at Alexandria with the West.

The charter granted, the Orange and Alexandria Company was organized May 9, 1849, and surveys were undertaken to determine the exact route the O. and A. was to follow. Actually, two surveys were made. One group started from Alexandria and the other from Gordonsville, but the resulting proposals encompassed two completely different routes. When the two factions eventually compromised, neither group was satisfied, for not only was the route inefficient from an engineering point of view, but also it by-passed Warrenton and Fairfax, two important commercial centers of the day. However, under the compromise, it was agreed that a branch line would be built to connect Warrenton with the main line.

Construction was started at Alexandria early in 1850, and was completed as far as Manassas Junction by October 1851. By November 1852, the road was operating as far as Culpeper, and by March 1853, as far as Gordonsville, where it connected with the "Virginia Central Railroad" (the former Louisa line), which had at that time been completed from Richmond, through Gordonsville, to Lynchburg. By 1861, the Virginia Central had been extended through the Blue Ridge Tunnel to Staunton, and on almost to Covington. Thus, prior to the outbreak of the Civil War, the Shenandoah Valley was united with the seaport of Alexandria. And it was said that as early as 1860, no wheat farmer in the Valley had to transport his crops by wagon as much as fifty miles in order to ship them to Alexandria, Baltimore, or Richmond. Hence, the economic impetus of the railroad was tremendous, and proved a boon to Fairfax County as well as to the port of Alexandria and the Shenandoah Valley.

About the time construction had begun on the O. and A., the General Assembly granted a charter to the "Manassas Gap Railroad Company," permitting construction of a line from Manassas Junction to Harrisonburg, by way of Strasburg. Construction, begun at Manassas Junction in 1851, was completed as far as Strasburg three years later, and as far as Mount Jackson in 1858.

Originally, the Manassas Gap line leased O. and A. trackage rights to Alexandria for the sum of $33,500 annually. This financial burden was too great, however, so the company decided to build its own line into Alexandria. Once the appropriate surveys were completed, the

Electric Depot, Fairfax

Railroad Station at Clifton

necessary property rights were acquired. Although much of the grading was completed and many of the bridge abutments were built, the track was never laid, for increasing financial difficulties curtailed construction. With the outbreak of the Civil War, construction was stopped completely, never to be resumed. Today, many of the bridge abutments still stand as a memorial to the hopes of the men who set out to build across Fairfax County a major link in the Nation's transportation system. And the route the tracks themselves were to have followed is still apparent, for much of the original fill and grading are intact.

During the early stages of construction of the line to Alexandria, the directors of the Manassas Gap line had enthusiastically envisioned a branch into Loudoun County, from which they expected to go on to the coal fields of Hampshire and into Paddytown on the north branch of the Potomac. Here, too, the financial difficulties, and eventually the war, thwarted the hopes of the would-be empire builders. Shortly after the line was surveyed and grading was begun, the work was halted permanently.

Both the O. and A. and the Manassas Gap lines suffered severely from the alternate depredations of Union and Confederate Armies. Three of the O. and A.'s sixteen locomotives were captured immediately. Station buildings and water tanks were wrecked, and the Bull Run bridge was destroyed and rebuilt seven times during the war years. The Manassas Gap line lost locomotives and other equipment, and its property, too, was severely damaged.

Once the war was over, the Manassas Gap Railroad was absorbed by the O. and A., and the new line thus formed was renamed the "Virginia Midland Railroad." During the Reconstruction period, rolling stock and equipment were obtained on credit from the United States Military Railroads, and the line prospered. But construction was never resumed on the additional lines originally planned by the Manassas Gap Railroad.

In 1894, upon formation of the Southern Railway System, the Virginia Midlands Railroad became the northernmost segment of the Southern's main line, and, as such, the route is still being operated today.

Although its trains did not run through Fairfax County until after 1870, the "Richmond, Fredericksburg and Potomac Railroad" was the first rail line to influence the county's transportation facilities. The R. F. and P. was chartered in the 1830's as a rail-steamer line, with trains running from Richmond through Fredericksburg to the mouth of Aquia Creek, at which point passengers and freight were transported by Potomac River steamer to Alexandria and thence to Washington, Baltimore, and other ports. The line had imported nine wood-burning locomotives from England and when service was inaugurated in 1836, passengers gasped at their breath-taking speed of ten miles an hour. Over this combination rail-steamer line, the traveler could speed from Richmond to Washington in less than twenty-four hours, which was in those days an amazingly short time for the distance traveled.

Operation of the line was curtailed during the Civil War, of course. But once regular service could be resumed, the ravages of war were repaired rapidly, new equipment and rolling stock were acquired, and new wharves were built at Quantico Creek to replace those at Aquia Creek. From Quantico, steamers continued to transport passengers and freight to Alexandria and Washington.

In 1870, the Pennsylvania Railroad acquired control of the "Alexandria and Fredericksburg Railroad," a short line which had been chartered in 1864. The line was to have provided service between Alexandria and Fredericksburg, but it had never been built. Under the ownership of the Pennsylvania Railroad, the Alexandria and Fredericksburg line was completed and service was begun on it on July 18, 1872. From Fredericksburg, the Pennsylvania used the R. F. and P. tracks to transport goods and passengers to Richmond, so service between Washington and Richmond was available on either of the two trunk lines -- the Pennsylvania or the R. F. and P.

Eventually, dissension arose between the two lines, for the Pennsylvania's directors objected to the R. F. and P.'s continuing steamer service from Quantico to Washington. As a means of exerting economic pressure, the Pennsylvania discontinued its traffic to Quantico, thus reducing the R. F. and P.'s traffic to Richmond, and the R. F. and P. was forced to accede to the Pennsylvania's demands and discontinue steamer service. Once this was done, amicable relations were restored.

In 1890, the Pennsylvania Railroad merged the short "Alexandria and Washington Railroad" with its "Alexandria and Fredericksburg Railroad." Renamed the "Washington and Southern," the new line continued to connect with the R. F. and P. at Quantico.

In 1901, the Pennsylvania, the Southern, the Chesapeake and Ohio, the Sea Board Air Line, the Atlantic Coast Line, and the Baltimore and Ohio joined together to form the "Richmond-Washington Company." The new company acquired all of the stock of the Washington and Southern line as well as a majority of the voting stock of the R. F. and P., and operated the two lines as separate entities. Then, in 1920, the Washington and Southern ceased to exist when it was merged with the R. F. and P. The latter has continued to operate under the same name and is the only railroad serving Fairfax County (in fact, one of the few in the United States), which has retained the name under which it was originally chartered.

It is interesting to note, also, that the Commonwealth of Virginia was an original stockholder in the R. F. and P., and that after more than a century of producing dividends, the stock is still yielding a satisfactory return.

Railroad Station at Great Falls

Mount Vernon

Life on the Great Plantations

The plantations of early Virginia were basically self-sufficient. Each was run pretty much as a community unto itself, with agricultural techniques and the domestic arts and crafts passed down through the generations by the masters and mistresses and servants.

The arrangement of mansion and outbuildings followed pretty much the same general plan throughout the Colony. The main house, usually referred to as the "great house," would contain from eight to thirteen rooms, the size of each being more important than the actual number. Outbuildings near the main house were detached, yet were closely related to the domestic life of the mansion. Nearest the house was the kitchen, sometimes connected by a covered passageway which the servants used in transporting the great dishes and platters of food bound for the family dining room. One entire side of the large kitchen was devoted to the open fireplace and the ovens, where the cooking was done.

Nearby was the wash house, and next to it the storehouse, from the rafters of which hung the famous smoked hams and the bacons. At the opposite end of the mansion were the shoemaker's house, carpenter shop, and schoolhouse. Under the eaves of the outbuildings were the sleeping rooms of the servants.

Farther away from the mansion were the coach house and stables, and beyond them the dairy house. For the great homes there was often a grist mill, and sometimes a planter had more than one. Washington had a grist mill on Dogue Run Farm at Mount Vernon and another one up the river.

The upkeep of the plantation required many servants as well as field laborers. Before the Negro was brought to the plantation, the English servant was brought either on a voluntary basis at a regular salary, or by a contract under which he agreed to work for a specified period in exchange for his passage to the Colony, and other gratuities. The contract usually required that at the end of his service he be given a pair of shoes, three barrels of corn, and farming tools. Sometimes he also received fifty acres of land. With this start, the indentured servants eventually became prosperous landowners, so the contract was beneficial to both parties, and employers were assured of a stable labor situation under which they could make long-range plans.

When Washington first established his home at Mt. Vernon, he asked a friend in Philadelphia to get for him "a joiner, a bricklayer and gardener." Two of his indentured servants went off in a small yawl and he advertised for them in a Virginia paper, offering $20.00 reward each for their return.

The planters spent their days overseeing the proper operation of their property. In addition to managing the house and household servants, the mistresses became physician and nurse. Some even studied cures and provided all the medication the family and servants needed. But their resources were limited, and family burial grounds reflected a high mortality rate.

A common affliction of the gentlemen of the family was the gout, and a form of discomfort felt by all was the inflammation caused by the wood tick, which flourishes today just as it did then in meadow grass and forests.

Social life in the early days of the Virginia Colony centered around the home, and most of the social life was geared to family activity and family participation. A large family was a social necessity and the men and women of the day married young, while neither widow nor widower retained the solitary status for long. Weddings, christenings, and funerals were events that brought relatives and friends from a distance as well as those that lived nearby.

The plantation house was ideal for large gatherings, for it usually had a good-sized reception room off the central hall, and, in some cases, a large ballroom. On the whole, the people were fun loving, generous, and hospitable, and everyone was welcomed, from the casual caller to the relative whose visit extended a lifetime.

Washington is said to have compared Mt. Vernon to a "well resorted tavern." And many a planter complained that the cost of his hospitality was driving him to bankruptcy. The warmth of the welcome never wavered, though, and rather than refuse hospitality outright, a planter would abandon his large home and build in a more remote area, where visitors came less frequently.

At the plantation homes along the riverbanks, the exchange of visits between the planters and the captains of the clipper ships was enjoyed by all. The planters depended upon the ships' captains for all types of information from England, including news of Parliament and the Court, and the latest in politics, scandal, and small talk. While the families were pleased to welcome the sea captains, it was also often a relief to see the ships leave, for while the captain made himself at home in the great houses, the crew made themselves unpopular everywhere else, committing petty thievery and starting fights.

The arrival of one traveler was a mere trifle, and even a coachful did not create a hardship, for servants were numerous and food, grown on the plantation, was plentiful. So balls and parties were not always restricted to a single night or day, but often lasted four or five days. Some of the guests stayed continuously, making the occasion a house party, while others went back home overnight, then perhaps returned to the party again. The dances popular in Colonial days were minuets, giggs and reels, and country dances.

There were but few holidays, and those which were observed were usually religious ones. Christmas was the time of principal celebration among family groups.

In the earliest days, there was little formal education. Alexandria developed its Academy shortly after the Revolution, and the turn of

Ash Grove. The main part of the house was built in 1790 by Thomas Fairfax, son of Bryon, Eighth Lord Fairfax. Located in the Tyson's Corner area, on Ash Grove Lane in McLean, Ash Grove is the only surviving house of those built by the Fairfax family during the eighteenth century.

Birthplace of General Robert E. Lee

Stratford—*from a silkscreen print by Ruth Starr Rose. Built about 1725-30 by Thomas Lee, Stratford overlooks the Potomac in Westmoreland County. The mansion is in the form of the letter H and is entirely unlike others of the Colonial South, having been built to conform to a plan much favored in England in Elizabethan and Jacobean times but never adopted in Virginia. A robustly masculine structure, Stratford was a fitting home for thirty-two distinguished descendants of its builder. Thomas Lee, the only native Virginian to be appointed by the Crown as governor of Virginia, was himself a notable statesman, and among the members of the Lee family who once lived at Stratford are governors of Virginia, members of the Council and of the House of Burgesses, two signers of the Declaration of Independence, the foremost cavalry officer of the Revolution, and the brilliant and heroic General Robert E. Lee.*

the century saw the establishment of the Episcopal Theological Seminary and the Episcopal High School, as well as Coon Cottage, the finishing school established by Dr. and Mrs. Baker in Fairfax on property near Truro Episcopal Church.

Before that time, education of the children was largely in the hands of tutors brought over from England or Scotland. Some were young ministers and other were indentured servants. The tutor would often supplement his teaching by keeping the planter's accounts.

Resident tutors were employed by General Washington for Mrs. Washington's grandchildren. The first tutor was Gideon Snow, who was followed by Tobias Lear. Both also acted as secretary to the General. Washington wrote of the tutor's life with the family: "He will sit at my table, live as I live, mix with the company who resort to my house and will be treated in every respect with civility and proper attention. He will have his washing done in the family and may have his linens and stockings mended by maids in it."

In Colonial times the young girl's education went no further than her private tutor could take her, but her early training was slightly more intensive than her brother's. In addition to academic learning, she was expected to acquire such other accomplishments as musical skills, knowledge of sewing and embroidery, and methods of home management which would enable her to become a good housekeeper. The girls married young and usually left home as brides at about the same time the young men of the family left for the university.

Established in 1693, William and Mary College was the first neighboring university available for sons of the Virginia planters, and residents of both Virginia and Maryland were taxed for it at the rate of a penny per hogshead on all tobacco exported to England. Up until the Revolution, the sons of the wealthier families were usually sent to England for college training.

Most plantation homes boasted fine libraries, and since the children had a great deal of leisure time, they were encouraged to read. The books of the day required great concentration and deep thought, and provided young readers with a basic code of ethics as well as general information that helped build character.

Christ Church (from the Brady Collection of the Library of Congress)

St. Mary's Church

Pohick Church

Religious Life in the Early Days of the County

The religion of the day also helped to produce good men and women with sound ethics, for it was profoundly devotional and seldom controversial. From the beginning, the Episcopal Church was the state church and represented a picturesque but vital element in the life of the people until the Revolution knocked away the political props by repudiating the state-supported church.

During the Colonial period, the religious aspects of plantation life were quiet ones -- the church was an easy part of an easy life. The richer and more influential planters organized themselves into a small, close corporation in the vestry, which represented the social directory of the neighborhood. Clergymen frequently came to Virginia direct from England, freshly ordained, and became sincere, devout powers in their parishes.

In Colonial days, failure to attend church services was made a civil misdemeanor and the offender was punished by the state. Later, a shilling was the penalty assessed for missing service. Actually, the offender suffered by being absent, for in addition to missing the religious message, he also missed the gossip, the fashions, and the sociability which were important adjuncts of church attendance.

Describing the Pohick Churchyard, a Mr. Davis, who tutored at Occoquan, writes: "A Virginia Church yard on a Sunday resembles rather a race ground than a sepulchral ground; the ladies come to it in carriages and the men after dismounting from their horses make them fast to trees. But the steeples to the Virginia churches were designed not for utility but for ornament, for the bell is always suspended to a tree a few yards from the church."

The uses of bells were many. Oftentimes, people resting comfortably in the high-backed pews of the churches had a tendency to nod, especially when the collection was being taken. At the end of the reaching rod on the collection bag hung a small bell that was tinkled as it came to the drowsy ones, making them uncomfortably conspicuous.

Since clergymen were paid in tobacco, certain parishes were at a disadvantage, for a parish that raised poor tobacco seldom had a good preacher. In addition to the salary, the churches provided clergymen with living quarters on church-owned property called "glebes," which the clergymen were permitted to farm as a means of augmenting the usually meager salary. Despite the additional income, some of the clergy were forced to turn to teaching as well as farming to eke out a living.

Many of the churches of Colonial days were simple rectangular buildings, handsomely built, and trimmed with two tiers of windows. The pulpit was raised on a high support so the minister could be seen and heard by all. The high-backed pews were privately owned and passed from generation to generation in the same family. The galleries that were added later were usually occupied by the servants.

The Pohick Church was established near Occoquan Creek in the late seventeenth century. In 1732, it became the parish church of Truro Parish, which was created by the Virginia General Assembly that same year. Presumably a wooden structure, the church was located some two miles southeast of the present Pohick Church, although the exact site is not known.

By the 1760's, the old church had deteriorated to the point where it was decided by the vestry to erect a new building at a new location. Among the vestrymen of Truro Parish were George Mason, George William Fairfax, and George Washington. The present site of Pohick Church was selected largely at the urging of George Washington, who preferred the new location because it was nearer Mt. Vernon. Throughout his lifetime, Washington always kept two adjacent pews at Pohick Church, so as to accommodate his house guests as well as members of his family.

A contract was made with Daniel French to erect the new building on approximately three acres of land which had been purchased from him. Following the plans drawn by James Wren, French began the work in 1769 but died before the church was completed. George Mason then took over the job of "undertaker," which was the eighteenth century term for "contractor." The church was completed and the first services held in it in 1774.

While the walls of the present building are the original ones, the interior has been rebuilt. A close reproduction of the original, it was recreated to replace the interior destroyed during the Civil War when the church was successively occupied by Confederate and Federal troops.

Pohick Church is an active congregation of the Episcopal Diocese of Virginia and holds three services each Sunday. The church is located at the intersection of U. S. Route 1 and Telegraph Road, six miles from Mt. Vernon. It is open to visitors daily from 9:00 a.m. to 5:00 p.m. There are no governmental contributions of any type for maintaining the church, and no charge is made for admission, but donations from visitors are accepted to help pay for the upkeep of the buildings.

The original Falls Church was named for the Little Falls of the Potomac River, which were nearby. The town, later established around the church, took its name from the old church.

The first Episcopal Church on the site was built in 1733, and was known as the "upper church." It was a wooden structure that cost 33,500 pounds of tobacco and was built by Richard Blackburn of Rippon Lodge, the man who designed the original portion of the Mt. Vernon mansion.

In 1735, Augustine Washington, father of George Washington, became a vestryman of the parish which included the church. He nominated as rector the Mr. Charles Green, who made a trip to England for ordination to Holy Order, and then became the first rector of the parish.

Francis Scott Key, author of the "Star Spangled Banner," once served the church as layreader, and George Mason, author of the Virginia Bill of Rights, was elected to the vestry of the parish in 1748.

An addition to the old church was undertaken in 1760 but a few years later the vestrymen found it unfit for repairs. So on March 28, 1763, they resolved to build a brick church at the same place. The new church was planned, complete with galleries, and was designed and constructed by Colonel James Wren. Begun in 1767 and completed and accepted by the vestry in December 1769, the Colonial red brick building is the same one in which the congregation worships today.

On April 25, 1765, the Truro Parish had been divided and Fairfax Parish created. The original Falls Church then came under the new parish. The present church was thus planned by the Truro Vestry, but was built by the Fairfax Vestry.

George Washington had been appointed one of the vestrymen of the parish in 1762 and he and George Mason and George William Fairfax were on the building committee of The Falls Church.

The plan used for The Falls Church was followed generally in the building of both Pohick Church and Christ Church, which were completed in 1772 and 1773, respectively.

The Falls Church has had long periods of neglect as well as periods of loving care. There have been four major restorations: in 1823, 1866, 1905, and 1959. The 1959 restoration under the rectorship of the Reverend J. Hodge Alves, was the most extensive, and at that time the north wing was added. Also, the interior was completely redone, with sanctuary, galleries, and a narthex added.

The church is located at 115 E. Fairfax Street in the City of Falls Church and is open to the public from 8:00 a.m. to 5:00 p.m. daily.

Another important church was Payne's Church built in Truro Parish in 1766, after the congregation had met for about a year in a tobacco warehouse owned by Samuel Littlejohn.

Edward Payne was commissioned to build the church along the lines of the Falls Church for a fee of 579 pounds, Virginia currency. The site was on land owned by Mr. Thomazen Ellzey, near Ox Road (now Route 123), a short distance from the present site of the Fairfax County Courthouse. Mr. Ellzey is said to have given a glebe of forty acres nearby, from which the rector was to be allowed to keep whatever he could grow, as a means of augmenting his salary.

Payne's Church was used regularly by the Episcopal congregation until about the time of the Revolution, after which it was used only intermittently. The Baptist Church acquired the property early in the nineteenth century and the church was used by the Baptists until 1840, when the denomination was divided. Then the Jerusalem Baptist Church was organized and used the building until 1862.

Federal troops, camped in the Fairfax area during the Civil War, demolished the church, tearing it down brick by brick and using the material in building their winter quarters. After the Civil War, a small frame church was built on part of the original foundation of Payne's Church.

In 1753, the Truro Vestry ordered the Pohick Church rector to hold services in Alexandria on every third Sunday. Apparently the services

St. Timothy's Episcopal Church, Herndon

The Falls Church

were held in a building loaned by a parishioner, for the vestry books of the period show records of payments for furnishings for the church, but nothing for the building until plans were made for the present structure, which was completed in 1773. Though the church was originally under the control of the Truro Vestry, Christ Church, along with The Falls Church, came under the control and management of the Fairfax Parish when Truro Parish was divided in 1765.

Christ Church is often described as the church at which Washington worshipped. Actually, it was at Pohick Church that Washington worshipped for the greater part of his life, and technically, he was not a member of the Fairfax Parish which controlled Alexandria's church affairs after 1765. However, as Washington's life became more and more involved -- during and after the Revolution -- he found it more convenient to worship at Christ Church and purchased a pew there.

Christ Church is also in regular use today -- bringing to a total of three the number of churches established in Fairfax County in Colonial days that have continued to thrive to the present day.

Located at 118 North Washington Street in the City of Alexandria, Christ Church is open to visitors from 9:00 a.m. to 5:00 p.m. on weekdays, and from 2:00 p.m. to 5:00 p.m. on Sundays.

Payne's Church (from a photograph taken in 1861)

Thomas, Sixth Lord Fairfax

Thomas, Sixth Lord Fairfax

When Thomas, Lord Fairfax, returned in 1747 to make his home in Virginia, he lived for several years with his cousin, William Fairfax, at Belvoir, the first manor house constructed in Fairfax County. Located near the mouth of Hunting Creek on land purchased from Dr. Charles Green, Rector of Truro Parish, the red brick, two-story house was sixty by thirty-six feet and boasted a full basement. On the main floor were a large central hall and four rooms, while upstairs there were five large bedrooms.

William Fairfax had begun the building of Belvoir in 1741, and when the complex of buildings was completed in 1743, it included, in addition to the manor house, numerous brick outbuildings -- offices, stables, and coach house.

William Fairfax's daughter was married to Lawrence Washington, then owner of Mt. Vernon, and the Washingtons and Fairfaxes often visited together. Since young George was living with his older brother, Lawrence, while Lord Fairfax was residing temporarily at Belvoir, the two became well acquainted, and, despite political differences, remained life-long friends. It was during the first year of Lord Fairfax's residence in Virginia that Washington, then only sixteen years old, surveyed the entire Fairfax Proprietary. Washington's only assistant in the complicated surveying project was George Fairfax, the son of William Fairfax, who was a young man of about Washington's age. Lord Fairfax was so pleased with Washington's work that he had him appointed a public surveyor.

After considering various locations on his vast domain, Thomas Fairfax eventually selected as the site for his new home, a sloping stretch of land eleven miles southeast of Winchester in what is now Clarke County. When it was completed in 1752, Lord Fairfax called his home "Greenway Court," after the ancestral seat of the Culpepers in Kent County, England.

Much of Lord Fairfax's time must have been required for the management of the Northern Neck (or the Fairfax Proprietary, as it came to be called), but from all available accounts it seems that he still found time to enjoy life as a Colonial gentleman.

For almost forty years Greenway Court was the scene of lavish entertainment as Lord Fairfax surrounded himself with his favorite friends. He was, however, an eccentric man who made no effort to conceal his dislike of ladies, and it is said that no woman was ever admitted to Greenway Court. Another evidence of his eccentricity lay in the fact that although he seemed to enjoy his home in all other respects, he did not choose to sleep there but usually slept in a small outbuilding.

The gentlemen of the Colonial period dressed in lavish fashion, and, while some historians declare that he was disdainful of dress, Lord Fairfax kept an elaborate wardrobe. According to an itemized account, he had on hand during one season:

"One velvet suit, and other suits in brown, blue and drav; scarlet and green silk coats; scarlet laced, green damask laced, and gold tissue waist coats; and scarlet plush and black velvet breeches."

In his conduct, character, and appearance, Lord Fairfax appears to have remained the typical English aristocrat throughout his life. He also remained a Loyalist and a Tory, but since he took no active part in the Revolution, he was not harmed.

The William Fairfaxes were Loyalists too, and at the outbreak of the Revolution, they went to England to live. Belvoir was destroyed by fire near the end of the war, and William Fairfax and his wife decided to remain in England, despite repeated urgings from George Washington that they return to Virginia and rebuild their home.

Thomas Fairfax is said to have taken to his bed upon the news of Cornwallis' surrender at Yorktown and to have died soon thereafter. Whether the British defeat played any part in his final illness is debatable, however, for he was an elderly man at the time of his death.

Lord Fairfax is buried in a crypt at Christ Church in Winchester. Not far from his burial place, on display in the shenandoah Valley National Bank in Winchester, is the ponderous iron chest Lord Fairfax brought from England. Undoubtedly one of the most interesting Colonial chests in Virginia, it weighs several hundred pounds and has an unusually beautiful lock of lovely scrollwork design.

Also on display in the bank is a copy of the estate account of Colonel Thomas Bryan Martin, one of the executors of the estate of Thomas, Lord Fairfax. The account reads in part:

"1798, Sept. 25   By cash contained in an iron chest found in the house of Thomas B. Martin Dec'd and which has been delivered by Robert Dunbar to Robert Macky and was found to contain Seven Hundred and Thirty Crowns; Eighteen Thousand Eight Hundred and Seventy Three Dollars and Eighty Cents; Cut silver Three Hundred and Seventy and an half ounces; English and Portuguese gold Two Hundred and Fifty Six ounces Eighteen and an half pennyweight; Spanish Cob Gold Sixty Three ounces and Two pennyweights; French and Spanish Gold One Hundred and Thirty Seven ounces and Eleven and an half pennyweights; German Gold Fifty ounces and Twelve pennyweights, amounting to, as credited by Robert Macky, 8682 Pounds, 3 Shillings 7-1/2 Pence."

The Code Duello

The Code Duello provided gentlemen of the so-called "old school" a means by which they might settle their differences on the field of honor. In many cases, the code brought to a violent end the life of one or the other of the participants in the duel.

In the North, the code lost its popularity shortly after Alexander Hamilton was killed in a duel. But affairs of honor continued to be conducted with some frequency in the South, and even increased after the Civil War.

In Virginia during the 1700's, duels were commonplace -- perhaps because many of the young men returning from English universities brought back with them some of the Old World concepts. Another factor that encouraged dueling was the migration to the Colonies of British and Continental officers well schooled in the theory that gentlemen resolved personal differences by their own methods.

Dueling had no formal rules until the 1800's, but the usual procedure was for the offended party to issue his challenge in writing, through a friend, naming the time and place that satisfaction would be sought. The place was usually a creek or river bank, cemetery or churchyard. The challenged man then had the right to choose the weapons and the distance at which they would be used. Having made these arrangements, the seconds would draft in detail a formal statement of the conditions under which the affair of honor would be conducted. At the appointed time, the participants would take their positions, with surgeons in attendance to care for the injured, and then the duel would begin.

In 1779, Thomas Jefferson proposed to the Virginia Legislature that a law be passed which would, among other provisions, make the death penalty the mandatory punishment for anyone who killed another while dueling. The law was enacted in 1796, but many loopholes were found. Under the law, those who had participated in duels or who had borne challenges were to be barred from holding public office, but for a number of years, successive legislatures waived such political disbarment.

In 1808, the Congress of the United States outlawed recourse to the duello by Army personnel. Neither Congressmen nor Army personnel bothered to pay any attention to the law, however. While duels over political matters were common, they often were fought as the result of rivalry over a pretty girl, too.

There was so much dueling before 1880 and such concerted efforts to stop it, that would-be duelists were forced to play hide-and-seek with the law. Often all participants were arrested, turning the affairs into comedy situations rather than the tragedies they might otherwise have been.

One of the more publicized duels was that of John Randolph and Henry

Clay. A place near the Little Falls on the Virginia side of the Potomac was selected for the duel, so that in the event Randolph should fall, he might die on Virginia soil. There were two exchanges of fire in the duel, but no harm was done except that Clay sent a fiery ball through the tail of the elaborate dressing gown his opponent was wearing.

The Code Duello finally died out in Virginia in the late 1800's.

General Washington's Tomb (Courtesy of the Mount Vernon Ladies' Association)

George Washington of Mt. Vernon Plantation

Fairfax County's most famous citizen of all time was George Washington. Born in 1732, he was the son of Augustine Washington, a Virginia planter, and the great-grandson of John Washington, an Englishman who emigrated to the new world in 1657.

Although Washington's education was limited to elementary subjects, he had an exceptionally keen mind and acquired a good knowledge of mathematics and surveying, chiefly by self-study. As a young man, Washington wanted to enter the British Navy. But, heeding the wishes of his mother, he gave up the idea and instead became a surveyor. At the age of nineteen, however, he was appointed Adjutant General of the Virginia Militia, and even though a military career was no longer a part of his plans, the appointment marked the beginning of a long period of distinguished military service.

Washington was among the volunteers who accompanied General Braddock on his disastrous expedition in 1755, and was almost the only officer who returned safely from it. In 1758 he took an important part in the expedition that captured Fort Duquesne, where Pittsburgh now stands.

In the meantime, as the result of the death of Lawrence Washington, his half-brother, Washington had come into possession of the Mt. Vernon estate. Shortly after his return from the French and Indian Wars, Washington married Mrs. Martha Custis, a widow with two children who had become the charming belle of the Vice-regal Court of Williamsburg. The wedding was held at St. Peter's Church, near the bride's home in New Kent County, Virginia, on January 17, 1759. The following spring the couple took up residence at Mt. Vernon.

Immediately, the new owner instituted plans for improving the estate. He added many acres to the already large estate and built new outbuildings and a large, sixteen-sided barn of brick and wood which was a wonder of the day. In managing the estate, Washington was not satisfied to follow what were considered conventional methods, but was constantly devising new and better procedures for performing the varied work on the plantation. He adopted the system of crop rotation later recommended by Thomas Jefferson, and planted orchards of the best fruit then known, obtaining the best seed and stock available. He managed his estate with the same systematic planning that had distinguished his military career.

When the Revolution began, Washington was chosen unanimously as Commander-in-Chief of the Continental Army. He had loved his life at Mount Vernon, and during the long, weary years of the Revolution, he kept the thoughts of Mount Vernon in his mind as an oasis.

Finally, Washington was able to return to his beloved home. But before long, he was again called to serve his country. In the spring of 1789, he was notified that he had been unanimously chosen President of the United

States. And so again he prepared to leave his home. After placing his house in order, Washington journeyed to Fredericksburg, fifty miles away, to share the news with his mother. It was at this time that she told him that she felt that when next he returned to Virginia, she would no longer be living. She urged him to go, however, and to "fulfill the destiny which heaven appears to have intended for you."

Washington was inaugurated as the first President of the United States on April 30, 1789, and in 1793 he was elected for another four-year term. The advances made by the young republic during the eight years of Washington's leadership were extraordinary. But once his two terms as President were completed, Washington turned his energies from affairs of State to the less arduous activities of plantation owner.

Once more in residence at Mt. Vernon, Washington continued with his plans for improving and enlarging his estate. Returning one evening in December 1799 from a day of supervising the work on the plantation, he complained of a chill. The next day, December 14, he took a turn for the worse. As evening fell, he gently passed away, surrounded by his sorrowing household and medical attendant. To those about him he said, "I am going, but I have no fears."

George Mason

George Mason of Gunston Hall

By the American people in general, George Mason is best remembered as the author of the Virginia Declaration of Rights, from which evolved the Bill of Rights that comprise the first ten amendments to the Constitution of the United States. By the people of Fairfax County, he is also remembered as an eminent statesman and one of the county's most outstanding citizens of all time. Unfortunately, details of his personal life are comparatively unknown, for he kept no diary, did not write an autobiography, and his personal correspondence is widely scattered.

A fourth generation Virginia aristocrat, George Mason was born in 1725 at Mason's Neck, Virginia. His forebears as well as his descendants served in public office and his father, a Knight of the Golden Horseshoe, was among those who accompanied Governor Spotswood across the Blue Ridge.

When George was only ten, his father was drowned when his sailboat capsized while he was crossing the Potomac. The boy's education was left to his mother and a kinsman, Colonel John Mercer. He did not have a formal education, as did his younger brother, Thomson, who was sent to England to study law. But the desire for learning was sparked by his guardians, and George learned much through self-study.

George Mason was a life-long friend of George Washington, and the two often visited together, either at Mt. Vernon or at Gunston Hall, where George Mason made his home after his marriage to Anne Eilbeck.

Mason was a modest, rather retiring individual, who probably would have preferred to live simply on his plantation, enjoying the companionship of his wife and nine children. However, he was called upon repeatedly to serve the Virginia Colony, and his personal ability coupled with his wealth and high social standing made him one of the most influential Virginia planters of the day. He was identified with many Colonial enterprises and became a member of the Virginia House of Burgesses in 1759.

In 1764, with the passage of the Stamp Act, the Colonies became indignant. George Washington, also a member of the House of Burgesses, requested Mason to prepare a bill to provide means for avoiding the use of stamped paper. This Mason did, and the bill was then introduced into the House of Burgesses by Washington. The reaction was so strong that in 1766, the Stamp Act was repealed.

Mason's opinions and assistance were again sought by Washington in 1769, when the Townsend Act was passed by Parliament, placing heavy taxes on many imports. Mason answered with the "non-importation" resolutions, which were also introduced in the House of Burgesses by Washington. As a result of Mason's efforts, the Townsend Act was repealed in 1770.

Feeling against England was running high following Parliament's passage of the "Intolerable Acts" in 1774. Washington was so incensed that when the Boston Tea Party took place, he threatened to raise a thousand men and march to the aid of Boston. Mason's reaction to the "Intolerable Acts" was the formulation of his famous "Fairfax Resolves," in which he summarized the grievances of the Colonies. The first clearly written statement defining the Colonies' rights in relation to England, the "Fairfax Resolves" were adopted by the Virginia Legislature in August of 1774 and became known as the "Virginia Resolves." Later, they were adopted by the Continental Congress.

Upon the adoption of the "Fairfax Resolves" by the Colony of Virginia, Mason and Washington established procedures through which they could act for Fairfax County in the event of emergency. Mason evolved the plan for creating the first organized militia in the Colonies, the "Fairfax Independent Company of Volunteers," and Washington became its first captain.

Mason was a delegate to the Virginia Convention of 1775 and was re-elected in 1776. At this convention, held in Williamsburg, all ties with England were severed. The primary purpose of the convention was to prepare a "Declaration of the Rights of Man," and it was as a delegate to the convention that Mason drew up his famous "Virginia Declaration of Rights," which was adopted by the convention on June 12, 1776, and became the basis of the Declaration of Independence as drafted later the same year by Jefferson.

The Virginia Constitution, which Mason wrote, is the first "written constitution of a free commonwealth." Jefferson, writing in 1825, said, "The fact is unquestionable, the Bill of Rights and the Constitution of Virginia were drawn originally by George Mason, one of our really great men, and of the first order of greatness."

Mason was chairman of a committee set up for the purpose of designing a state seal, and the present seal, with the motto "Sic Semper Tyrannis," was the result.

In 1785, Mason was appointed commissioner for Virginia and asked to arbitrate the controversy between Virginia and Maryland over navigation rights on the Potomac. This meeting led to the Convocation at Philadelphia in 1787, which framed the Constitution. Mason did not sign the Constitution and openly campaigned against its ratification in Virginia because he opposed a central government with unfixed powers. He wanted to limit the powers of the legislative branch of the government as well as to limit the terms of office of the President and members of the Senate. He favored the gradual abolition of slavery and desired to incorporate into the Constitution a "declaration of rights." At the Virginia Ratifying Convention, when other patriots joined him in his fight, his efforts were successful. It was Mason's phraseology which was used in the "subsequent Amendments," or "Bill of Rights," which were introduced in Congress and became law on December 12, 1791.

Declining an appointment as United States Senator from Virginia, Mason returned from Richmond and retired to Gunston Hall, where, on October 7, 1792, he died. In his will on file at Fairfax Courthouse is his message to his sons:

"I recommend it to my sons from my own experience in life, to prefer the happiness of independence and a private station, to the troubles and vexation of public business, but if either their own inclinations or the necessity of the times should engage them in public affairs, I charge them on a father's blessing never to let the motives of private interest or ambition induce them to betray, nor the terrors of poverty and disgrace, or the fear of danger or of death, deter them from asserting the liberty of their country, and endeavoring to transmit to their posterity those sacred rights to which themselves were born."

Gunston Hall, completed in 1758, was the third Manor House to be built in Fairfax County. William Buckland was brought from England to design and build the mansion, which is located at Lorton, fourteen miles south of Alexandria, off U.S. Route 1. The famous boxwood gardens were planted in 1758 and were restored by the Garden Club of Virginia in 1953. The mansion was restored and furnished by the National Society of Colonial Dames of America and is open to the public daily.

Robert "King" Carter

"King" Carter's Copper Mine

During the period from 1715 to 1728, various persons in quest of land and the minerals that might lie beneath, were exploring Virginia. Starting from the Rappahannock, they went up the Shenandoah Hunting Path, then eastward into the vast forest which would some day be known as northern Fairfax. As a result, large grants of land were patented by various individuals and groups along the several branches of Cub Run.

After the first influx of settlers came the sons of the fabulous Robert "King" Carter, who, in his own right, had earned a remarkable reputation as a Colonial official, landholder, and the agent of the fifth Lord Fairfax. At the age of twenty-eight, "King" Carter had entered the Assembly as a Burgess from Lancaster County and had served five years, becoming one of the most prominent members of the Assembly. After the death of Virginia's Governor Drysdale in 1726, Carter was, for a few months, acting governor.

It was in 1702 that "King" Carter became the agent for the Fairfaxes, and he served in that capacity for twenty years. It was a strategic position in which to seek to acquire a fortune, and Carter made the most of it. He has been described by Fairfax Harrison, author of Landmarks of Old Prince William, as a man of "tremendous energy, shrewd business habits, dominant personality and accustomed to success in whatever he undertook." Possibly it was because of the great power he exercised that he received the name of "King." He was known as a generous man, too, and at his own expense he built Christ Church in Lancaster County. The tombstones of Carter and his wives, who are buried in the churchyard at Christ Church, were described by Bishop Meade in 1838 as probably the largest, richest, and heaviest in the United States.

Carter had two wives. The first, Judith (Armistead), died in 1699. The second, Elizabeth (Landon), died in 1710. The children of both marriages married into the first families of the Colony, and, as a result, Carter had a great number of distinguished descendants, including two who became Presidents of the United States, and six who became governors of Virginia, as well as another distinguished descendant -- General Robert E. Lee.

One venture in which the great "King" was not successful was his attempt, through the "Frying Pan Company," to find and mine a vein of copper ore in Fairfax County. His sons, Robin and Charles, had pushed deep into the interior of the county and then east to Horsepen Creek off Broad Run. On Frying Pan Creek, a small run emptying into Horsepen Creek, the Carter brothers discovered a generous showing of the characteristic green sandstone of Northern Virginia. Certain that this was a rich deposit of copper, Robin obtained a grant for the land. A few months later, on March 17, 1728, to be exact, a contract was entered into by "King," his sons, and his son-in-law, Mann Page, agreeing that the

Chain Bridge, showing high water during the spring flood, March 19, 1936.

land should be exploited for the mutual benefit of the parties concerned.

The company planned to build a road to the Little Falls of the Potomac as the shortest route from the mine site to tidewater. But before arrangements could be made, the plan was revealed to Thomas Lee. Intent on protecting his own commercial plans -- whereby he hoped to obtain a monopoly of the navigable headwaters of the Potomac -- Lee entered a hasty survey in the proprietor's office, claiming all available landing places at Little Falls. He thus cut off further plans of the Carters. The "King," accustomed to having his own way, proceeded to bombard Lee with correspondence wherein he alternately raged at him and then turned to flattery. But the "King" was unsuccessful and finally was forced to look elsewhere for a landing. Eventually, he and his partners decided to build a wharf on the Occoquan. They opened and extended an old Indian trail all the way to Frying Pan Run, past what later became the site of Payne's Church and the present Fairfax Courthouse. This is how the present Ox Road (Route 123) came to be established.

The Frying Pan Company controlled in all some 27,000 acres of land, including the tract at the Occoquan landing and a half-way station on Ox Road. Having opened the mine, hopes ran high and the company imported Cornish miners to direct the Colonial laborers. But, unfortunately, the samples sent to assayers in London and Bristol brought unfavorable reports, and what Robert Carter had attempted this time, had to be acknowledged to have come to nothing.

Although the Frying Pan Company's mine was abandoned, the name "Frying Pan" lived on as the name of the creek, then the town, and also the old church which still stands today on Ox Road.

The origin of the name "Frying Pan" is obscure. According to one legend, it came from the fact that when the miners left the area after the operation folded, they left behind a frying pan, and from that incident the name was derived. Another legend, which presumably pre-dates "King" Carter's time, is that a band of Indians had encamped overnight at the run and in the morning they missed their frying pan. Hence, the name was conferred to the place at which the frying pan was lost.

However it came about, the settlement on Frying Pan Run was first known as Frying Pan. Later the name was changed to Floris, and this is the name the town bears officially today -- although many area residents still refer to it by its former name.

Potowmack Canal Locks, Great Falls

George Washington's Potowmack Canal Project

A transportation dream which ended as a financial failure was George Washington's "Potowmack Canal Project."

The Potowmack Canal was a project to which Washington devoted much time, and, as a favorite business enterprise, the canal ranked second only to Mt. Vernon in Washington's affections.

During the years he was engaged in surveying work, Washington had a good opportunity to become familiar with the Potomac River. Studying the area over a period of years, he conceived the idea that the falls might one day be by-passed by a canal which could constitute a major artery of commerce between the Northern Virginia area and the Western wilderness.

When Washington returned to Mt. Vernon after Cornwallis's surrender, he again turned his interest to the canal project. In 1784, he outlined in a letter to Virginia's Governor Harrison a plan that was undoubtedly the first major public improvements project in the Nation's history. At the same time, he proposed a bill for incorporating a company which would open the Potomac to navigation. The bill was passed by the Virginia Legislature almost immediately. But because Virginia had granted the Potomac waters to Maryland, it was necessary to have Maryland's cooperation for any development of the river. So, in the fall of 1785, Washington invited James Madison and representatives of both Virginia and Maryland to come to Mt. Vernon and discuss the complex question of commerce among the states of the Confederacy. At this meeting, known as the Mt. Vernon Convention, Articles regarding commercial interests were drawn up between Maryland and Virginia.

Another convention was proposed for the following year at Annapolis, and all the States of the Confederacy were invited to send representatives. Here, they discussed commercial relations not only along the Potomac but also throughout the new Nation. At the close of the meeting, Alexander Hamilton proposed that another conference be held -- this time in Philadelphia. As a result of the Philadelphia Convention, the Constitution of the United States was drawn up.

Meanwhile, Washington had become president of the canal company and supervised construction of the canal from 1785 until he was again called into service to the Nation in 1789.

Together with General Richard Henry Lee, "Lighthorse Harry," Washington envisioned at a strategic point on the canal, near the edge of the river, a city which they hoped would become a major metropolis on the trade route from the western frontier. The city was to be named "Matildaville," in memory of General Lee's first wife.

Contemporary records show that the locks at Little Falls were reported as being complete in July 1795. A report made by John Mason

Potowmack Canal Locks

(one of the canal company's directors) to the Secretary of the Treasury on January 20, 1808, describes the locks as follows:

"At the Great Falls are five locks.
  One length 100 feet, width 14 feet, lift 10 feet
  One length 100 feet, width 12 feet, lift 11 feet
  One length 100 feet, width 12 feet, lift 14 feet
  Two length 100 feet, width 12 feet, lift 18 feet
  Construction blown out of solid rock
  Distance, including a Basin, 1200 yards.

"The sluice gates in these locks are deep. They do not lift but are made of cast iron and turn on a pivot fixed in the center."

Of the original five locks, only two remain in fairly good condition today. In lock number two are to be seen the trademarks of the individual stone cutters -- symbols representing an ancient tradition introduced by the artisans from Europe. In 1920, when the White House was restored, similar markings were found in the original stone walls of the Executive Mansion. Each mark has its own meaning and many of those in the White House walls were identical to those in the locks, indicating that the same artisans may have worked on both projects.

Low water hampered operation of the Potowmack Canal, so comparatively little freight was hauled through it during the three decades it was in use, and the tolls collected varied from $2,000 to $22,500 a year.

In 1798, the Potowmack Canal Company's board of directors met in Georgetown to consider the fate of the project. It was obvious that the canal would never become a money-making project, so the directors decided to abandon its operation. Thus, Washington's dream was declared a financial failure. The failure was a magnificent one, however, for this was the first canal project attempted in the new Nation. A forerunner of the Chesapeake and Ohio Canal which carried freight on horse-drawn barges from 1828 to 1924, the Potowmack Canal remains the most impressive engineering feat in our Nation's early history.

Potowmack Canal, Great Falls

Chimney from Mrs. Myer's Tavern (later called Dickey's Inn) at Matildaville. The inn, which served as a retreat for all United States Presidents from George Washington to Theodore Roosevelt, was destroyed by fire in June 1949.

Matildaville

A few stone ruins are all that remain today of the town named in memory of Henry Lee's first wife, Matilda. They stand near the Great Falls of the Potomac on an eighty-acre tract in Fairfax County that is leased by the National Parks Service for recreational purposes.

The granddaughter of Thomas Lee and the daughter of Philip Ludwell Lee, Matilda was described by her contemporaries simply as "divine." No portraits remain to show what Matilda Lee looked like, nor are there any letters which might give a clue to her personality. It is known, however, that when "Light Horse Harry" Lee decided to visit the home of his cousin at Stratford, Matilda Lee "took his breath away."

After his graduation from Princeton, Lee was placed in command of a cavalry company in Virginia and served in the Continental Army under Washington's immediate control. While Lee's company never numbered more than three hundred men, it became the flower of Washington's troops. The men were brilliant in action, impeccable in dress, and as swift as foxes on their missions. Their tasks were to spy on the enemy and to capture supplies. Speed was an essential ingredient for their survival, so the men were equipped as lightly as possible. Thus, General Lee's nickname of "Light Horse Harry" derived from the fact that his military outfit always traveled light.

Lee's fame increased as the war progressed and he was among those present when Cornwallis surrendered his sword to Washington. With the Revolution over, Lee returned to Leesylvania, yearning only for the peace and solitude of home. But he was too active to remain in solitude long, so Lee shortly decided to visit his cousin at Stratford. He knew that upon the death of Philip Ludwell Lee, Stratford had passed to the oldest child, Matilda. But he was not prepared for the loveliness of the nineteen-year-old Matilda, who, with her sister Flora, greeted him upon his arrival at Stratford. Less than a month from the time Lee journeyed to Stratford and met Matilda, the two were married.

Matilda was a wife with expensive tastes, but she could well afford to be, for she had not only inherited Stratford with its six thousand acres of rich tobacco land, but also other lands throughout Northern Virginia. Inventories tell that her side saddle cost twelve hundred pounds of tobacco and that her music lessons on the harpsichord cost 3,330 pounds of tobacco.

Harry took Matilda with him when he represented Virginia in Congress and their years together were gay and happy. Then, suddenly, their happiness was at an end. Matilda was dead at twenty-six years of age, leaving Harry to raise two children -- Lucy Grymes, born in 1786, and Henry, born in 1787. Harry brought his young wife home to Stratford and buried her there at the foot of the garden.

Some years later, "Light Horse Harry" Lee stood with George Washington on the site of the proposed town near the Great Falls of the Potomac -- the town which the two hoped would be a strategic point on a major trade route to the West. The two men decided to name the town "Matildaville" in memory of the lovely woman whose life had been so brief.

There was no planning commission for Matildaville, but certain requirements regarding construction of dwellings were set up. The Potowmack Company established its headquarters at Matildaville and maintained shops, a forge, and a superintendent's residence there, as well as barracks for the laborers. A grist mill and a saw mill were also established.

The Virginia Assembly issued a charter for the town in 1790, and named as trustees a group of prominent citizens interested in the establishment of the town. Included among them were George Gilpin, Albert Russell, William Gunnell, Josiah Clapham, Richard Bland Lee, Leven Powell, and Samuel Love.

The tract on which the town was located was originally part of a grant of 5,468 acres patented from the Northern Neck Proprietor by a John Colvill, one of the wealthiest men in the area at that time. In 1797, Bryan Fairfax, Rector of Christ Church, leased to "Light Horse Harry" Lee a large tract which circumscribed the property on which the town was located.

The forty acres comprising the town were subdivided into lots, and streets were laid out. Among the street names were Washington, Gilpin, Lee, Fairfax, and Canal. Tobias Lear, who was employed as a secretary by Washington during his retirement, purchased six lots. He was one of the many who hoped the property would develop into a valuable business enterprise.

However, the span of time during which the town was active was a comparatively short one. When the Potowmack Company was abandoned, the town had no further reason to exist and, before long, lapsed into obscurity. The ruins remain today only as a historic site and as a tribute to a lovely lady.

Ruins of the old jail at Matildaville

Woodlawn Plantation

Eleanor Parke Custis, better known as Nelly Custis, was one of four children left fatherless by the death of John Parke Custis, son of Martha Washington by her first marriage. The two older daughters went to live with their mother when she remarried, but Nelly and the son, George Washington Parke Custis, remained at Mt. Vernon and became the wards of Martha and George Washington.

At this time Washington was busily engaged with the destiny of the young republic, and hence could not spend a great deal of time with the children. Nelly and George Washington Parke Custis adored him, however, and spent a happy childhood at Mt. Vernon.

The children were an attractive pair and Nelly grew into a charming and delightful young lady. She was taught all the social graces of the day, including the art of playing the harpsichord. She sang Washington's favorite songs and helped entertain his distinguished guests, among whom was General Lafayette.

When she was nineteen years of age, Nelly became engaged to Major Lawrence Lewis of Culpeper County, the son of Washington's sister. As a special compliment to George Washington, Nelly chose February 22, 1799, for her wedding date.

Major Lewis was a favorite nephew, so, as a wedding gift to the couple, Washington announced that he had set aside 2,000 acres, including part of his Dogue Run Farm, the grist mill, and the distillery, which they were to inherit upon his death. Although he asked them to stay on at Mt. Vernon to assist in entertaining the constant flow of visitors, Washington urged the Lewises to start building on the land he had set aside for them.

William Thornton, the first architect of the Capitol, designed the manor house which was built on the 2,000 acre tract and which was named "Woodlawn," for Major Lewis's childhood home.

Completed in 1805, the Woodlawn mansion is of red brick which was fired on the plantation, trimmed with local Aquia stone. Considered a typical example of late Georgian design, the central unit is flanked by pavilions connected by low structures called "hyphens." The facade on the river side is famous for its portico columns of handsome design, its marble floor, and its double stairway.

Nelly adjusted easily and gracefully to her duties as a lady of the manor, and for nearly forty years she maintained a gracious hospitality at Woodlawn. Among Woodlawn's famous guests was General Lafayette, who returned to the United States in 1824 and, renewing his acquaintance with the lovely Nelly, visited her and her husband in their own home.

There were eight children born to Nelly and Lawrence Lewis, four boys and four girls. Two were born while the Lewises were still residing at Mt. Vernon, the other six at Woodlawn.

Eleanor Parke Custis, better known as Nelly Custis.

Nelly died in 1852, thirteen years after her husband's death, and is buried at Mt. Vernon near the resting place of her guardians.

Woodlawn passed out of the Lewis family in 1846. Changing hands several times, the mansion went into a gradual decline and at one time stood vacant. A series of owners after 1900 spent large sums of money on its rehabilitation, and when the estate was again offered for sale in 1948, the Woodlawn Public Foundation, Inc., was set up to raise funds to purchase the property and to restore and refurnish it. Since 1951 the estate has been managed by the National Trust for Historic Preservation, and was the first property accepted by the organization after it was established in October 1949 by an Act of Congress. A non-governmental, non-profit organization, the National Trust for Historic Preservation is empowered to receive "donations of sites, buildings, and objects significant in American history and culture, to administer and preserve them for public benefit."

The interior of Woodlawn retains the charm of the typical Virginia plantation home, with spacious rooms carefully furnished with excellent pieces from the eighteenth and early nineteenth centuries -- many of which were possessions of the Lewis family. The woodwork is painted in imitation wood-grain, as was the fashion in the early nineteenth century, and the colors used throughout the house are those selected by Nelly Custis Lewis.

The mansion clearly reflects the interests and personality of Nelly Lewis, for many mementoes of her life at Mt. Vernon as well as her years at Woodlawn are on display. Her music lies open on the pianoforte, and unfinished bits of her exquisite needlework are near a favorite chair. Exceptionally fine examples of American samplers and quilts are displayed, as are historic pictures and maps of the mansion and plantation.

Under the supervision of the Garden Club of Virginia, the gardens and grounds have been restored as accurately as existing records permit. The boxwood near the entrance was probably started from cuttings from the bushes at Mt. Vernon, and one of the ornamental rose beds is copied from Mt. Vernon, the other from Tudor Place, the Georgetown home of Nelly's sister which was also designed by William Thornton.

Woodlawn is open to the public daily (except January 1 and December 25) from 10:00 a.m. to 5:00 p.m. A nominal admission fee is charged.

Woodlawn

Sully

Sully

In his will, Henry Lee of Leesylvania left to his sons, Richard Bland and Theodorick, "my lands in Loudoun." This included what later became known as Sully, for the plantation was in Loudoun County at that time but was returned to Fairfax County in 1798 when the boundary line between the counties was changed.

Richard Bland Lee, then twenty-six years of age, was the older and therefore was allowed his choice as to which half of the property he wanted. He chose the northern half, where the Sully house now stands.

In 1788, Richard gave to Henson Lewis a "three lives lease," in which it was stated that a house of certain dimensions must be built on the land within seven years. The stone house standing today at Sully might have met the requirements of this lease, but historians believe the stone house either is a patent house or that it may have been the Lee's "quarters" house.

Since Richard Bland Lee at one time represented Loudoun County in the House of Delegates, it appears that he was then living on his father's land, and it is probable that at that time he built the log house at Sully. When Liza Collins went to Sully as the bride of Richard Bland Lee, she wrote of the "honeymoon cottage," a log house Richard had built.

Richard was Northern Virginia's first representative in Congress and attended the sessions when Congress met in Philadelphia. There he met and fell in love with the charming Liza Collins, the daughter of a Quaker importer and merchant living in Philadelphia. After their marriage in 1794, Richard brought his bride home to a large log house which, until about 1870, stood about three hundred yards east of the present Sully house.

A description of Sully -- the Colonial frame house that Richard built later -- is given in a letter written by Liza's father to her mother. Only a portion of the letter was preserved, but it reads as follows:

". . . They are obliged to go more than three miles to get sand to make mortar for the new house, which is nearly all done but the plastering and painting and the piazza across the front. It is a very clever house, has an elegent hall 12 feet wide and a handsome staircase and two very pretty rooms on the first floor. One is 19 by 20 feet and the other 20 feet by 17. There is two large and one small chamber in the second story and one handsome and large chamber in the third or garrett story, nearly square with a large window in the gable and another good lodging room besides. Indeed it is and will be a very neate handsome house.

"The kitchen is about 60 feet from the house and is a finer one than is in twenty miles square and it is in fact a kitchen and laundry

Child's bed that has been in the Lee family for years is considered the most valuable piece of furniture at Sully.

with a very handsome chimney with cranes in them. Indeed it is properly speaking a compleate double kitchen or kitchen and washhouse and on each end of the . . . "

This is the end of the portion of the letter preserved. But further description is given in a letter which is dated October 24, 1797, and headed Sully, from Thomas Lee Shippen to his father:

"This is the seat of Mr. R. B. Lee in Loudoun County, 27 miles from Alexandria, 25 miles from Dumfries and 50 miles from Fredericksburg. We arrived here yesterday from Leesburg before dinner and the great importunity of this delightful family persuaded us to pass this day with them, when it promised to be like yesterday, a fine one. It has turned out a very bad one and it rained harder than I have seen it rain these many months. Happy travelers to have such a shelter from the storm. I would fain give you some idea of the elegence in which this kinsman has settled himself to make amends for the caprise of his fellow citizens ---. The house is new, built by himself about three years ago, and lately furnished in Philadelphia with every article of silverplate, mahogany, Wilton carpeting and glassware that can be conceived of that you will find in the very best furnished houses in Philadelphia, parlours and chambers completely equipped with every luxury as well as convenience.

"Mr. Lee's family is composed of his lady and son three months old. Portia and Cornelia Lee, who have made choice of him as may have heard, on the death of their Uncle Frank, as their guardian and the young Turberville who is a branch of our family."

Portia and Cornelia Lee grew up at Sully. Still in existence are many letters written by the two sisters after they had grown and left Sully, and the letters show that the girls regarded Sully as home.

It is interesting to note that General and Mrs. Washington were godparents of Richard Bland Lee, Jr., who was born at Sully. Also, that Liza Collins Lee and Dolley Madison were lifelong friends, and that Liza served as a bridesmaid for Dolley at her first marriage. The Lee Society has more than a hundred copies of letters written to Mrs. Lee at Sully by residents of the White House, Mt. Vernon, Woodlawn, Ossian Hall, and other famous homes.

Richard Bland Lee was a leader in the building of the Little River Turnpike and was one of the twelve gentlemen who set up the town of Middleburg, although he was not a resident there. Also, he was one of the men who worked to bring about the change in the boundary between Loudoun and Fairfax Counties, which returned Sully to Fairfax County. The same bill that provided for the transfer of the portion of lower Loudoun to Fairfax also provided for the establishment of Fairfax Courthouse in its present location.

Among the private enterprises in which Richard Bland Lee was involved was the Lee family quarry at Aquia Creek, which provided some of the stone used in building the Capitol and the White House.

The East Room at Sully

On February 1, 1811, Richard Bland Lee sold Sully to his nephew, Francis Lightfoot Lee, son of Richard Henry Lee. Francis Lightfoot Lee was later judged to be incompetent, and Richard Bland Lee was appointed his guardian.

In 1839, Sully was sold to William Swartout, who was said to have been a pirate and an admiral in the Texas navy. Supposedly, he was arrested in Virginia, turned over to English authorities, returned to England, and hanged as a pirate. However, no record has been found of his having been an admiral or of his having been hanged in England. It appears that Swartout actually came to Sully from Mississippi, bringing with him many servants but no family. He lived a life of seclusion, occasionally taking trips that lasted weeks or months. It also seems probable that he died at Sully about three years after purchasing the property.

The Sully plantation was sold about 1842 to Jacob Haight, a Quaker from Duchess County, New York. The house and a part of the land became a present to a daughter, Maria Haight, some years after her marriage to James Barlow. Jacob Haight, however, retained a life interest in Sully and continued to live there until his death.

The next owner of Sully was Conrad Shear, also from New York. Sully was then sold several times and eventually came into the possession of Walter Thurston, who was at one time Ambassador to Mexico.

The Sully house as it stands today is the original house -- not a restoration. Also, almost everything on the inside is original -- including mantels, staircase, doors, etc. During their occupancy, the Thurstons installed modern plumbing and heating, but the room arrangement remains basically as it was when the Richard Bland Lees lived there.

Sully is located on the Dulles Airport-Sully Road, near U. S. Route 50 at Chantilly, and is open to the public daily from 10:00 a.m. to 5:00 p.m.

The Stone House at Sully, which historians believe was either a patent house or the Lee's "quarters" house.

Oak Hill

Ravensworth, Ossian Hall and Oak Hill

The history of Ravensworth, Ossian Hall, and Oak Hill is indeed an integral part of the history of Fairfax County, for the story of one is incomplete without the stories of the others.

Besides these three great homes, there was still another, called Cool Spring, of which only the old foundations and a spring remain today. Because it too was located on the Ravensworth plantation lands, Cool Spring undoubtedly played an important part in the history and development of Fairfax County, also. But little information is available today regarding its past.

The plantation which is the background for the four homes was granted to William Fitzhugh in the late 1600's. Fitzhugh had been born in Bedford, England, in 1651, and settled in Westmoreland County, Virginia. In 1685, he purchased from John Matthews (the original grantee) nearly 22,000 acres in what was later to become Fairfax County. Fitzhugh had the land surveyed in 1690 and then applied for a direct grant, which was confirmed in 1694.

Ravensworth Plantation had been named for an ancestral estate in England -- the seat of the Barons of Ravensworth. But it was not until the fourth generation of descent that some of the Fitzhugh family actually lived at Ravensworth.

The first William Fitzhugh had as tenants for this plantation, a party of French Huguenots, who raised tobacco on the plantation. It is probable that the next two generations of Fitzhughs continued the arrangements, since the leases arranged by William Fitzhugh were for the duration of "three lives," or three generations of lessees.

William Fitzhugh, Jr., of Chatham (great-grandson of the first William Fitzhugh) was the first of the Fitzhugh family to live on the Ravensworth Plantation, and it was he who built the Ravensworth mansion about 1796-1800.

Two other handsome homes were built on the Ravensworth Plantation about the same time. But Oak Hill and Ossian Hall, as they were called, were on that portion of the plantation to the north of Braddock Road which had been inherited by Henry Fitzhugh (brother of the grandfather of William Fitzhugh, Jr., of Chatham).

Ravensworth Mansion was to the south of Ossian Hall and Oak Hill and the approach was through an oak park. Ravensworth was a handsome home with a wide-pillared veranda extending the length of the main section of the house. Tubs of unusual shrubs and flowers decorated the veranda.

William Fitzhugh, Jr., of Chatham (later of Ravensworth) had two children: a daughter, Mary Lee Fitzhugh, who in 1804 married George Washington Parke Custis (Martha Washington's grandson) and went to live at Arlington House; and a son, William Henry Fitzhugh, who became

Ossian Hall

Ravensworth

a member of the Virginia Constitutional Convention and continued to be active politically throughout his life.

William Fitzhugh of Ravensworth died in 1809 and was buried at Ravensworth beside his wife, who had died four years before.

In 1830 it was rumored that the thirty-eight year old statesman, William Henry Fitzhugh, was headed toward the governorship, but death closed his career. He left a part of his estate to his adopted daughter, Mary Caroline Goldsborough, and the remainder went to his wife, Anna Marie, in trust for his sister, Mary Lee Custis and her daughter, Mary Ann Randolph Custis, who later married her childhood playmate, Robert E. Lee. To simplify legal matters for Anna Marie Fitzhugh, the Custises at that time relinquished all claim to the estate.

Prior to the death of William Henry Fitzhugh, the family had loaned their Alexandria townhouse to distant cousins, the widow of "Lighthorse Harry" Lee and her children. When she became ill, the Fitzhughs moved her from the townhouse to their mansion at Ravensworth, and it was there that Robert E. Lee went to see her in 1829 when he was called home from West Point because of her illness. She died shortly thereafter and was buried at Ravensworth, but many years later was re-interred with her husband ("Lighthorse Harry" Lee) and her illustrious son, Robert E. Lee, at the chapel at Lexington.

At the outbreak of the Civil War, Ravensworth was the refuge of Mrs. Robert E. Lee and her children, but she departed quickly from the home for the residence of cousins farther to the south so that her presence would not bring danger to Ravensworth.

When Anna Marie Fitzhugh died in 1874, she left the estate to Mary Custis Lee, who left it to her six children. Through the years, the land was gradually sold, but the mansion remained in the family until it was mysteriously destroyed by fire in 1925. The furnishings, which included heirlooms from the Lees, Custises, Parkes, Fitzhughs, and Bollings, had been removed before the fire, but many valuable paintings were burned. In 1957, the property was sold to a corporation for development.

The Henry Fitzhugh who had inherited the portion of Ravensworth Plantation on the north side of Braddock Road was a second cousin of the William Fitzhugh who had built the Ravensworth mansion about 1796-1800. Henry partitioned his holdings among his five sons, with the Ossian Hall portion going to Nicholas.

The exact date Ossian Hall was constructed is open to controversy. Eleanor Lee Templeman, author of Arlington Heritage, feels the date was later, but the late Senator Bristow indicated the mansion was built in 1735.

Ossian Hall was sold in 1804 to Dr. David Stuart, an Episcopal minister from King George County, who in 1783 had married Martha Washington's widowed daughter-in-law, Eleanor Custis. Dr. Stuart had studied medicine at Edinburgh and then returned to Virginia to make his home in Fairfax County. He became prominent in legislative matters and was active with his friend George Washington on the canal project at Great Falls. A member of the Virginia House of Burgesses, representing Fairfax

County, he was also the Virginia member of the three-man Board of Commissioners appointed by George Washington to decide the boundaries of the ten-mile-square area established as the site for the Federal City.

Mrs. Stuart died in 1811 and Dr. Stuart died in 1814. The estate then passed through various hands and in 1918, Senator Joseph L. Bristow of Kansas purchased the Ossian Hall mansion and the adjacent land and made it his home until his death in 1944. Members of Senator Bristow's family continued to live at Ossian Hall until 1951. Then the mansion stood vacant for some eight years, during which time vandals destroyed its interior with crowbars and hatchets. On September 3, 1959, the mansion was burned by the Fairfax County Fire Department to make way for a subdivision.

During the time he resided in Fairfax County, Senator Bristow had purchased various county farms as they became available and eventually he owned 4,300 acres. The parcel of land known as the "Bristow Tract" today comprises a number of major subdivisions, including Springfield, North Springfield, Bristow, Ravensworth Park, Monticello Forest, Ravensworth Farms, and West Springfield.

Of the four sister homes -- Oak Hill, Ossian Hall, Ravensworth, and Cool Spring -- only Oak Hill remains today. In design, Oak Hill resembled Ossian Hall, and it is probable that the two were built by the same workmen. Ossian Hall was two rooms deep, whereas Oak Hill is only one room deep on each side of the hall. But staircase, window frames, and much of the woodwork were identical. As was usual with Colonial mansions, Oak Hill originally had an outside kitchen, servants' quarters, and barns, as well as its own burial grounds. Very probably, the same was true of the other three mansions on the Ravensworth lands.

The Oak Hill mansion remained in the Fitzhugh family for a number of generations, and after the Civil War, it was owned by some Fitzhugh cousins named Battaille. Then the last of the Battailles left Oak Hill and went to live in the little schoolhouse in the woods, and for a time the mansion stood vacant.

Before the Civil War, a young Scotsman had been brought to the estate to act as tutor for the Lee and Fitzhugh children. When the war broke out, the young man, a Union sympathizer, fought on the Union side. When the war was over, he returned to Fairfax County and after the Battailles left Oak Hill, he and his Scotch bride moved into the mansion. Their youngest son eventually sold it to Mr. and Mrs. Edward F. Howrey, who live there today.

When the Howreys moved to the home in the 1930's, they found many souvenirs of the Civil War battles that had been fought on the Oak Hill estate. They also found in the attic many letters describing the period following the war when servants and field workers were gone and there was no food and no one to till the fields. Wads of Confederate bills were found stuffed under the floor boards and in back of old beams.

Aunt Lilly Newman, who had been born a slave and was the laundress for the Lees, lived in her own little house on a hilltop near Oak Hill.

It was she who gave to Mrs. Howrey the following account of the Oak Hill ghost, Miss Ann:

Prior to the Revolutionary War, Mr. Fitzhugh journeyed to England on business and took with him his pretty daughter, Ann. While there, Ann met and fell in love with a young English captain, Charles Hawkins. Then trouble began in the Colonies and Mr. Fitzhugh decided he should return to America to attend to his interests. His daughter, Ann, of course, returned with him.

Captain Hawkins, along with many other British soldiers, was sent to America to help put down the rebellion. The British landed at Dumfries and the Captain soon found his way to Oak Hill and his charming Ann. Welcomed by the Fitzhugh family, Charles Hawkins visited Ann many times. But then American troops learned of his visits and arrived unexpectedly one night and surrounded the house. Ann hid Charles in a secret room over the dining room, reached by a trap door concealed in a panelled closet. The Americans did not find Charles, but just as the troops were about to leave one of the soldiers stuck a sabre through the trap, killing not Charles but Ann.

Charles jumped through a fan light in the gable end of the house and escaped, and the grieving family buried their lovely young daughter. Legend has it that the blood stain on the dining room ceiling came back again and again, and that finally, to cover the stain, a tin ceiling was installed. The mansion acquired a name for being haunted by young Ann, who was said to be heard calling sadly for her Charles.

The legend remains today, and Mrs. Howrey says there is no accounting for the footsteps that are heard at intervals, and for the fact that doors which ordinarily stick, will suddenly and soundlessly swing open, seemingly of their own accord. When either of these phenomena occur, the Howreys merely say a polite "How-do, Miss Ann."

Mrs. Howrey admits that after hearing the story of the ghost of Oak Hill, she could not rest until she had crawled up into the secret room with a flashlight. There she found rusty red plaster covered over with tin, just as Aunt Lily had said. When Mr. Howrey inspected the ceiling, he discovered that the flashing around the brick chimney was rotten and rusty. He feels that a hard rain could have washed brick dust down on the ceiling, causing the red-brown stains to appear.

But the legend of the lovely young Ann and the ghost of Oak Hill lives on.

Maplewood on Route 123 near McLean, built by John J. Shipman in 1870, now owned by Mr. and Mrs. Rudolph Seeley.

Oakley, showing members of the Millan family

Oakley

Oakley, another Fairfax home dating back to Colonial times, faces what is now known as the Pender Road off Lee Highway, four miles west of the City of Fairfax. It was built about 1739 on property that was part of a tract known as Walker's Patent, which was a grant from the King of England to the proprietors of the Northern Neck. Exact records of ownership no longer exist, but it is known that the home and surrounding property were handed down through the years from one generation of the Millan family to the next, and that they were given to Colonel John Millan by his father, Thomas Millan, a Revolutionary War militiaman whose grave was marked a few years ago by the Fairfax Chapter of the DAR.

Colonel John Millan brought his bride to the home in 1810. Two years later, when the War of 1812 broke out, he raised a company of volunteers from among residents of the neighborhood and went off to fight. When the war ended, he returned and operated the farm until his death.

When the Civil War broke out, Colonel John Millan's widow was living at Oakley. She was quite an elderly woman and had with her only her daughter-in-law and three small children, the oldest of whom was only five. She was compelled to abandon Oakley and go to the home of a son in Rappahannock County. At an hour's notice, the widow left with her family just before the Battle of Bull Run, abandoning everything except such clothing and valuables as could be gathered quickly. Within an hour after she left, Northern troops took possession and ransacked the house. They were just about to set fire to it when a neighbor, a Northerner who had been befriended by members of the family, came upon the scene and persuaded the soldiers not to burn the house.

Captain John Quincy Marr, the first casualty of the Civil War, stayed at Oakley the night before his death. He and his company of one hundred men had camped in the yard and neighbors had carried in food and buckets of fresh milk for their supper and breakfast. The next morning the soldiers went on to Fairfax and the first military skirmish of the war.

General J. E. B. Stuart made his headquarters at Oakley for a time during the war, and it is believed Oakley was the campsite called "Qui Vive" of which John Esten Cooke wrote so vividly.

The Battle of Ox Hill, or, as it is also known, the Battle of Chantilly, took place on this property. After the battle, Union troops used the house as a hospital, and amputated arms and legs were stacked on the ground outside a first-floor window. The bodies of seventy-five soldiers were buried nearby in an old terrace garden covered with violets. The plants still bloom each spring in a profusion of blue and gray flowers -- perhaps as a living tribute to the soldiers who are buried there.

Miss Lillian W. Millan, who taught school in Fairfax County for forty-four years, was the last of the family to occupy the old home. Fairfax County purchased the property in 1952, but up until that time, it had always been in the Millan family. Part of the two hundred acre tract is now being used as a sanitary land fill, and a fire training station is being planned for another site on the grounds.

The James Wren House

James Wren was a resident of Fairfax County in the 1700's. An architect as well as a builder, records show that Wren was paid forty shillings for the plans furnished to the Vestry of Truro for Pohick Church, and that he also drew plans for Christ church, Alexandria, and was architect and builder of The Falls Church.

James Wren is believed to have been a descendant of the great Sir Christopher Wren, who was the architect of the Cathedral of St. Paul's in London, as well as the original building at the College of William and Mary in Colonial Williamsburg.

Little is known of James Wren's personal life, although records show that at one time he was a justice of the peace for Fairfax County and that he was a trustee of the stillborn town of Turberville, which was laid out near the Little Falls of the Potomac in 1798. It is known that in 1753 he married Catherine Brent. And it is believed that he married a second time, for in his will, dated March 9, 1808, and included in Fairfax County records, he devised to his wife, Sarah, a life estate in the tract whereon he lived, with the remainder of his possessions going to his son John. The small house in which he lived is still standing in Dunn Loring at 2606 Ogden Street. The house, a private residence, is owned by the Charles Bretschneider's, who live there with their family.

On a framed plaque hanging over the fireplace, the following is inscribed:

"This house of clap-board over brick, was erected in 1770 by Col. James Wren. Col. Wren used brick left over from the building of Falls Church (Episcopal Church) . . . 1765-69. He was the architect and builder of The Falls Church and his plan was used for Christ Church at Alexandria and Pohick Church near Mount Vernon. . . The real front of the house now faces the woods, not Shreve Road. The wing with the porch was added by the True family prior to 1945. This wing replaced a covered passage, additional wing, and outside kitchen. However, the brick floor of the passage was incorporated into the new wing. For the most part the house remains much as it was built. The one exception is the window frames. It seems one member of the family became a gambler and was not allowed to return home. Finally, full of repentance, he was allowed to return home by giving a gift of new windows for the house. The many old hand-made light windows were removed and the present Victorian Cross windows inserted. Especially handsome is the elegant cabinet in the dining room."

Fairfax County and the Civil War

Fairfax County received its introduction into the Civil War and sustained its first casualties during the early morning hours of June 1, 1861. From the forts outside Alexandria, Lieutenant Tompkins had come into Fairfax in command of a company of United States cavalry and charged through the small village firing shots at random into the air and at the homes of the sleeping inhabitants. Two Confederate cavalry companies were in the town at the time, one from Rappahannock County and one from Prince William County, and were camped in the courthouse enclosure. In back of the cavalry companies, in a field, were encamped the Warrenton Rifles, commanded by John Quincy Marr. One of the shots fired by Tompkins' men struck and killed Marr as he came from his tent to investigate the firing.

Ex-Governor William Smith, a man sixty-five years of age, had come down from Warrenton the day before to visit the Warrenton contingent and was spending the night with a friend, Joshua Gunnell. Upon hearing the commotion, Smith immediately went to the Warrenton group's campsite, and finding Marr missing, took charge of the company and marched the men down the pike leading through town. He encountered Tompkins' men and proceeded to deliver such a volley that they were sent to the foot of the hill at the edge of town. Smith realized this would not be the end of the incident, and he made preparations to give the Union soldiers a warm reception upon their return. The night was dark and the old governor told his men not to fire until the enemy was close enough that the heads of the horses could be seen. He placed the men along either side of the road and in a short time the Union cavalrymen again made their appearance. This time the fighting was in earnest and the casualties were many. But the raiders were finally driven from town.

After this encounter, the leader of the Warrenton Rifles became quite a figure on the fighting field, and with a dauntless courage served as an inspiration to the soldiers. He was seriously wounded at Antietam but was with the Confederate Army at Gettysburg. It was during this military campaign that Smith, for the second time, was elected governor of Virginia.

Also in Fairfax on that eventful early morning of June 1 was another man destined to become a leader of Confederate forces. He was Richard Ewell, who was on his way to place his services at the command of his native state. When Tompkins and his men entered the town and began firing, Ewell dressed hurriedly. As he came out into the street, he was wounded in the shoulder. He continued, however, to the camp of the Warrenton Rifles. Finding them in the capable hands of William Smith, Ewell returned to his hotel to take care of his wound.

Fairfax Courthouse, during the Civil War.

So the struggle which was to become a devouring flame began on Fairfax soil. And the name of John Quincy Marr was recorded in history as the first military man to fall in the conflict.

In the weary years that followed, Fairfax County felt all the heartaches and witnessed many of the horrors of the war. Located at the threshold of the Union Armies protecting the City of Washington, Fairfax County had scarcely a day in the next four years that some manifestation of the war was not apparent.

Union troops marched through for the First Battle of Manassas, and some were camped on Fairfax soil the night before. Following the battle, men and ambulances bearing the dead and wounded passed through the county on their way back to Washington. To a ridge in Fairfax County overlooking Bull Run Battlefield, came Congressmen and their wives and other prominent people of the social world, to witness what was thought would be the easy victory of McDowell's Army. But the scene turned out to be quite different from the one expected. About the time the victory celebration was to have started, Stonewall Jackson, who had been patiently waiting for the opportune time, thrust his brigade forward against the center of McDowell's attacking forces, and, with a quick, decisive bayonet charge, turned McDowell's troops back. It was a matter of only a short time when the retreat from Henry Hill became a panic, and those who had come to observe joined the retreating forces in a mad dash towards Washington.

The following year, the Second Battle of Manassas sent Pope reeling from the punishment inflicted by the troops of Lee and Jackson on August 28, 29, and 30. For a brief space, he rested on the heights of Centreville which had been occupied by McDowell previously. Jackson, however, gave Pope little time to pause, and on September 1, 1862, again struck at the rear of the Union forces at Chantilly (Ox Hill), three miles up the Little River Turnpike from Fairfax Courthouse, sending Pope back down the highways and through the fields of Fairfax to the forests near Alexandria.

Scars of the war were left deep on the area and probably no other part of the State suffered more. It was long after the war years that the county began slowly and painfully to rebuild.

At the close of the Civil War, two prominent Confederate officers lived in Fairfax County. Major General Fitzhugh Lee lived at "Clermont" and Brigadier General W. W. Mackall at "Langley." Several years later, General William Henry Fitzhugh Lee (known as "Rooney" Lee), the second son of General Robert E. Lee, also moved to Fairfax County and made his home at "Ravensworth," where he died in 1891. That same year, General Mackall died at Langley. General Fitzhugh Lee lived until 1901.

While General Robert E. Lee never lived in the county, he at one time owned jointly with his brothers, Charles Carter Lee and Sidney Smith Lee, a large tract of land at Fairfax Station.

Monument in Fairfax Cemetary honoring the Confederate dead.

Captain James W. Jackson and Colonel Elmer E. Ellsworth

Captain James W. Jackson, a native of Fairfax, was the proprietor of a popular tavern in Alexandria known as the Marshall House. He had been commissioned a captain in the Confederate service and authorized to raise a company of artillery. From the flagpole on top of his establishment, the Confederate flag floated proudly, and he had loudly declared that he would defend the flag with his life if necessary -- that any man who took it down would have to do so over his dead body.

Colonel Elmer E. Ellsworth arrived in Washington in August of 1860, in command of the Chicago Zouaves, whose colorful Algerian uniforms and unusual drills had inspired enthusiasm in many cities for the creation of similar companies. The twenty-four year old Ellsworth had become an intimate friend of the Lincoln family.

On the night of May 23, 1861, Federal troops crossed the river into Virginia, and Ellsworth's regiment was among them. Early the next morning, Colonel Ellsworth and a small body of men proceeded to the Marshall House to capture the Confederate flag flying from the rooftop. Ellsworth himself secured the flag, but as he descended the stairs, flag in hand, he was met by Jackson, who had been aroused from his sleep. Jackson, keeping his pledge, shot and killed Ellsworth. Private Brownell, who had accompanied Ellsworth, in turn killed Jackson. But before Jackson died, he is said to have grabbed the banner and wrapped the cherished emblem about himself.

Ellsworth's body was carried to a boat and taken across the river to a small house at the Navy Yard. The Lincolns, grief-stricken, arranged to have the funeral services held in the East Room of the White House. The event made a tremendous impression at the time, and there was city-wide mourning.

An inquest was held to determine the facts surrounding Jackson's death and the document summarizing the results showed that the people of Alexandria were unawed by the presence of Federal troops in the town.

Considering the intense feeling of the time, the document was a courageous one. It stated that an inquisition had taken place at the Marshall House in Alexandria on the 24th of May, 1861, and that jurors sworn to inquire when, how, and by what means the said James W. Jackson came to his death, had sworn upon their oaths that he was killed by an armed force of Federal troops while in defense of his hotel and his private rights.

Jackson's body was claimed and buried by his family. While there are no written records of the events, several legends are told as to what supposedly took place. One widely circulated story is that Jackson's widow and daughter removed his body to the grounds of Dower House, on Route 193 near McLean, where they buried it in a secret grave away from the Union soldiers who wanted to "string Jackson up" in a public place.

Dower House is said to have been built by Jackson and given to a daughter as part of her dowery. The Jacksons' home was some distance from Dower House, but according to legend, the soldiers mistook Dower House for the family home and set fire to it. Part of the house remained, however, including a portion of the stone chapel, and according to the story, the home was rebuilt. Then both mother and daughter were imprisoned as Southern spies. Upon their release, they returned to Dower House and made it their home.

Dower House was handed down through the generations to successive Jackson heirs, and finally became rental property of the estate. Former Attorney General and Mrs. Thurman W. Arnold took up residence in the house in the 1930's. One of their servants says that at certain times of the year, she and other members of the staff saw a ghost on the steps by the big gate near the lilac hedge and well. The ghost was that of a young girl wearing a little bonnet tied under her chin, sitting on the steps and sighing sadly. She is said to appear in the month of June, late at night, and supposedly is the ghost of Jackson's daughter, Jane. It is believed that she loved a Union soldier but did not marry him. So now she sits and sighs for her lost love.

Today the house is owned by a prominent Washington decorator, Donald D. McAfee. He has made some changes, but basically the house is in its original state. Mr. McAfee and his associate, Thomas Geiger, have added to the main structure a domed, all-glass greenery room which is entered through large glass doors leading from the dining room. With temperature and moisture automatically controlled, tropical plants flourish here. Mr. McAfee has also modernized the kitchen and altered the second floor somewhat to provide more closet space.

Although he has heard the many tales concerning the home, Mr. McAfee says that as yet he has not seen the ghost.

Mill, dating back to the early days in the County.

Fairfax Courthouse, showing monument honoring the memory of John Quincy Marr.

John Singleton Mosby

Mosby's Capture of General Stoughton

No history of Fairfax County would be complete without mention of John Singleton Mosby, one of its most colorful heroes. During the Civil War, Mosby's exploits were on the lips of Southerners and Northerners alike. One of the most daring was the capture of Union Brigadier General Stoughton at his temporary home in Fairfax.

About February 1, 1863, Mosby began operating among the outposts of the Union troops stationed in Fairfax and Loudoun Counties as part of the defense of Washington. During this period, Mosby had with him a detachment of fifteen men from Stuart's First Virginia Cavalry, then in winter quarters. The preceding year, Mosby had spent several months in Fairfax and had been on picket duty along the Potomac. He had, therefore, acquired considerable knowledge of the locality, and had been thinking for some time of making a raid on Fairfax Courthouse, for he knew there would be many military prizes to be taken there.

On the afternoon of March 8, twenty-nine men met Mosby at Aldie, in Loudoun County. He told only one of the men, Ames, that he planned to raid Fairfax. The others thought this was simply to be an attack on a picket post. It was late afternoon when they left Aldie. The melting snow on the ground muffled the sounds of the horses' hooves, and the drizzling rain that was falling brought an early darkness that concealed the men and horses.

The Union headquarters was so thoroughly girdled with troops that no one dreamed of the possibility of an enemy reaching the center of the camp undetected. And certainly, Brigadier General Edwin H. Stoughton had never conceived that anyone could have the audacity to pass by his pickets and ride right into his camp.

The names of the cavalry regiments stationed at Fairfax were familiar to Mosby, so whenever a sentinel halted his party, he answered, "Fifth New York Cavalry," which was one of the units actually there. Although Mosby and his men were dressed in Confederate gray, the night was so pitch black that it was impossible to tell from appearances to which side they belonged.

Proceeding to within a short distance of the courthouse, Mosby turned right and the little band of men slipped quietly into the town about two o'clock in the morning. With the exception of the two to whom he had confided his plans before they reached Fairfax, Mosby's men were completely surprised when they realized they were in a town filled with Union troops. Yet, there was no fear among them, for Mosby had never led them into a place from which he was unable to extricate them.

To a lesser man, and one uninitiated in the mysteries of nocturnal forays, Mosby's situation, surrounded on all sides by enemy troops, would have appeared desperate. But to Mosby it did not seem so at all.

Tour of Mosby's Confederacy

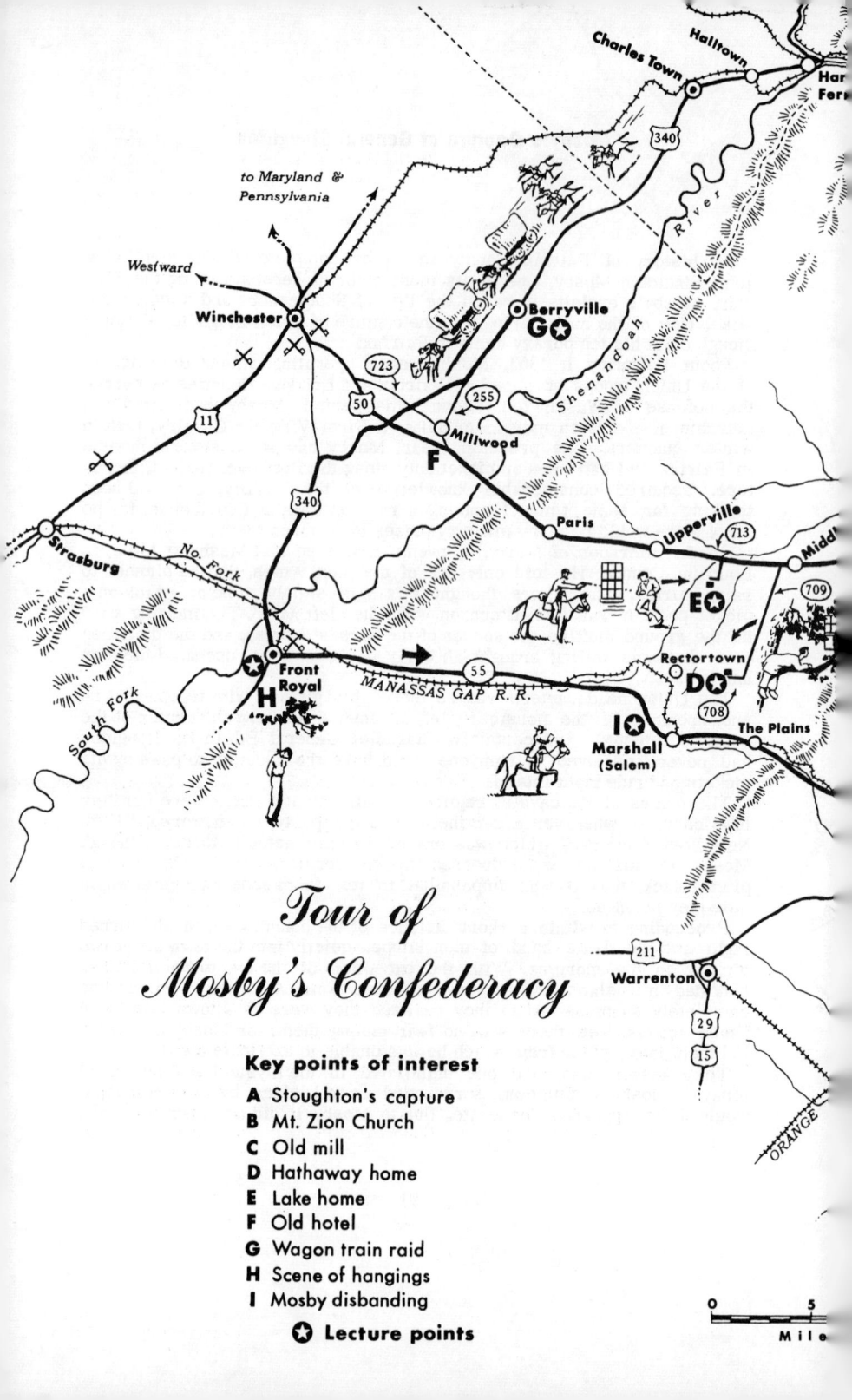

Key points of interest

- **A** Stoughton's capture
- **B** Mt. Zion Church
- **C** Old mill
- **D** Hathaway home
- **E** Lake home
- **F** Old hotel
- **G** Wagon train raid
- **H** Scene of hangings
- **I** Mosby disbanding
- ★ Lecture points

Drawn for 'Pat' Jones by Garnet W. Jex

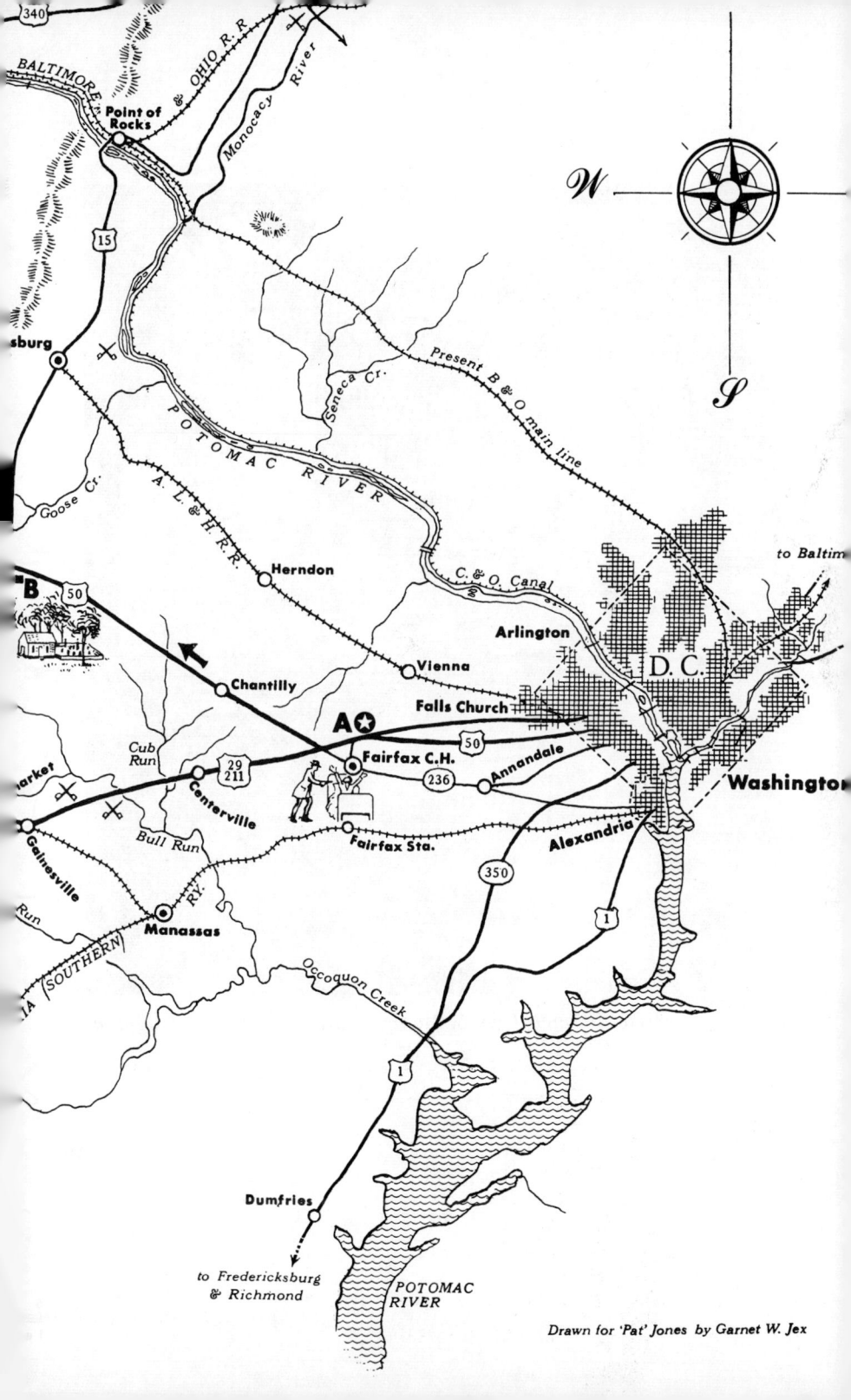

House in which Colonel John S. Mosby captured General Stoughton.

for previous experience had enabled him to measure the potential danger in such situations.

When they reached the courthouse square, the men were detailed into squads. Some were sent to the stables to collect the fine horses known to be there. Others were sent to various headquarters where officers were quartered. Actually, Mosby was more anxious to capture Colonel Percy Wyndham, Commander of the Union Cavalry, than any other, for Wyndham had been greatly annoyed by the midnight raids on his posts and embarrassed by his own unsuccessful attempts to capture Mosby.

A sentinel was walking in front of the building on Main Street which had been commandeered for use as a hospital. Mosby sent Ames to relieve the sentinel of his duty, and he himself went directly to the home of a citizen named Murray, which was believed to be Wyndham's quarters. This turned out not to be the case, however, and Mosby was told that Wyndham was at Judge Thomas's house at the other end of town. Quickly returning to the courthouse square, Mosby sent a band of men to Wyndham's quarters, but they found that the colonel had gone to Washington that evening by railroad. So Mosby's men compensated themselves for the loss by appropriating Wyndham's fine wardrobe and several splendid horses from the stable.

Next, they captured the telegraph operator who was sleeping in a tent in the courtyard -- they had cut the wires on their way into town. Mosby then took five men and set out to capture Stoughton, who was occupying the brick home of Dr. Gunnell on the outskirts of the village. Reaching the house, the men dismounted and gave a loud knock at the door. An upstairs window opened and a voice inquired as to who was there.

Mosby answered, "Fifth New York Cavalry with a dispatch for General Stoughton."

The door was soon opened by a man in shirt and drawers. Mosby seized him by the shirt collar and, whispering in his ear, told the man who he really was and demanded to be taken to the general. The astonished soldier led Mosby up the stairs, leaving the other men to stand guard below. Reaching the bedroom, Mosby struck a light and saw the great "man of war" deep in sleep.

The room showed signs of the frivolity of the previous evening, with unopened champagne bottles still sitting around. Mosby walked to the bed and pulled off the covering. Still the general snored on. Mosby then gave him a smart whack. The effect was electric, and the general rose from his pillow and, in an authoritative voice, demanded to know the meaning of the rudeness. Mosby calmly leaned over and said, "General, did you ever hear of Mosby?"

"Yes," the general replied quickly. "Have you caught him?"

"No," was the answer, "I am Mosby and he has caught you."

To add to the hilarity of the situation, Mosby then facetiously told the general that Stuart's cavalry held the town and that General Jackson was at Centreville.

The general dressed and then Mosby carefully led him out of the

*Plaque commemorating Mosby's exploit
Erected by the Fairfax Chapter, U.D.C.*

house, and they returned to the courthouse square, where the rest of Mosby's men had gathered.

Now there were prisoners and horses to cope with, and as Mosby and his men left the town, they took every possible precaution to avoid detection. Mosby knew that if he were to be caught, his career would be at an end, and it would be said that he had tried to do what he should have known was impossible. Yet, he was cheered by the knowledge that if he succeeded, the romance of this adventure would strike a deeper impression on the imaginations of men than if a battle had been fought and won.

Luck was with Mosby and again the sentry posts were passed in safety. So far as any of the sentinels knew, nothing had occurred to break the monotony of the cry, "All quiet along the Potomac tonight."

After passing the last Union outpost and traveling on several miles, Stoughton gave up all hope of recapture and release. He was a professional soldier and an ambitious man, and his pride was deeply hurt, for he knew that the manner in which he had been captured would subject him to ridicule.

Early the next morning, Mosby and his men reached Culpeper Courthouse with their captives: one general, two captains, thirty privates, and fifty-eight horses. During the day, Stuart arrived from Fredericksburg and was delighted when he heard the story.

Stoughton's reputation as a military man was ruined. He was soon exchanged but he never returned to the army. Wyndham was also relieved of duty.

Mosby was never able to duplicate the adventure, which has gone down in history as one of the most daring perpetrated during the entire war. It was of this audacious capture that President Lincoln is reported to have said, with his cynical humor, that he didn't care so much about the loss of the general, as he could make another in five minutes, but he hated to lose those horses.

The Rectory, where Mosby captured Stoughton, as it looks today.

The Burke Station Raid

J. E. B. Stuart's sense of humor was apparent even in the midst of heavy battle. The Burke Station raid that took place on December 26-31, 1862, was a perfect example of the general's combined skill and humor.

Stuart's wife, Flora, had arrived at her husband's camp to spend the Christmas holiday, and the commander's tent on Christmas Eve was the scene of merriment, with music, fine food, and the company of other wives as well as Mrs. Stuart. The countryside had been scoured for delicacies, so there was ample food for the occasion, including turkey, ham, sweet potatoes, eggs, and butter.

Although Stuart was outwardly cheerful and gay, he had already received marching orders from General Lee, who had planned a raid in force. Stuart said nothing during the evening's festivities, but before dawn on Christmas Day, he summoned his officers and informed them that they had only an hour in which to saddle and prepare to leave.

Stuart and the eighteen hundred soldiers proceeded to Kelly's Ford, eight miles from Culpeper, then rode on ten miles north of the Rappahannock and camped at the Village of Morrisville.

Their objectives were farther north and east, for they were to strike Telegraph Road (which was then the principal road connecting Washington and Fredericksburg) at Aquia, Dumfries, and Occoquan. They were then to move along the road, pick up any wagon trains or detachments of troops they met along the way, and do everything possible to alarm and confuse their Northern opponents.

Stuart planned a three-pronged attack on the highway: Fitz Lee was to cut the road on the south near Quantico; Rooney Lee was to hit Dumfries, five miles to the north; and Wade Hampton was to strike ten miles farther north at Occoquan. Under this plan the forces were expected to cut off a fifteen mile strip of the main highway and then unite.

Matters proceeded according to plan. Fitz Lee struck the highway south of Quantico. Rooney Lee came in south of Dumfries but found it heavily garrisoned. It was one of Colonel Candy's outposts and when the alert was given, Candy's brigade took up a strong defensive position outside Dumfries. The situation was reported to Stuart, who brought up Fitzhugh Lee's command, which was in the vicinity of Aquia and advancing north along Telegraph Road as planned. When Fitz Lee arrived at Dumfries, Stuart launched a dismounted attack against Candy with Rooney Lee on the left and Fitzhugh Lee on the right. Candy's forces, Stuart learned, were too strong for his own dismounted soldiers, so after a five-hour skirmish, he withdrew.

The command spent the night near the small hamlet of Cole's Store, where Hampton joined them with a few captured wagons and prisoners. Stuart sent the wagons, prisoners, and broken guns back across the Rappahannock during the night.

Meanwhile, Union authorities believed that all of the seven thousand cavalrymen belonging to the three brigades were with Stuart. The fact that Occoquan had been captured by Stuart and communications cut between Washington and the Army of the Potomac, caused great alarm in the Capitol and throughout the North.

The next morning, Stuart and his entire force moved from Cole's store toward Wolf Run Shoals. Then, learning that Wolf Run Shoals was held by a strong force, Stuart turned north and marched to Burke Station. He had learned that Colonel A. Schimmelfennig's infantry brigade and Colonel Louis P. di Cesnola's cavalry brigade of Stahal's XI Corps had pushed west of Stafford Courthouse after the wagons and prisoners were sent back. Stuart knew that it would be impossible to retreat by way of Morrisville and Kelly's Ford. He also knew that at Occoquan, Wolf Run Shoals, and Union Mills, brigades from Slocum's XII Corps held the fords across the Occoquan and Bull Run. Next, he discovered that Stoughton's brigade was at Fairfax Courthouse, that General Heintzelman had one brigade at Annandale, and that an additional brigade was moving in between Fairfax Courthouse and Annandale. Thus all routes of escape to the north were blocked.

Stuart planned his next move carefully. He gave out false information as to his own movements, and then, halting his men a mile from Burke's Station, had them close in quietly and swiftly on the railroad telegraph office. Stuart's men removed the operator from his key while he was still sending messages telling of the chase of Stuart's raiders. Then Stuart placed his own operator at the key, and, after receiving General Heintzelman's orders and checking on his map the location of Union forces, Stuart sent a message which became the classic joke of the times:

"Quartermaster-General Meigs
"United States Army
"Quality of the mules lately furnished me very poor. Interferes seriously with movement of captured wagons.
"J. E. B. Stuart"

Stuart then cut the wires, tore up the railroad, and set fire to the bridge across the Accotink. He moved north to Little River Turnpike before the gap between Annandale and Fairfax Courthouse was closed, and then moved north beyond Falls Church to Vienna. Continuing west to Frying Pan Church, his advance guard encountered Major Taggart, commander of the Union Cavalry outpost at Dranesville. Stuart attacked Taggart's squadron and drove it off.

Stuart and his men rested at Frying Pan Church and the next day marched to Middleburg, where they spent the night and then recrossed the Rappahannock and took up a position to the left of Lee at Culpeper.

General J.E.B. Stuart

J.E.B. Stuart at his Camp

It may seem difficult at first to picture the colorful General J. E. B. Stuart and his staff occupying Oakley. But in his book, Wearing of the Gray, John Esten Cooke, a relative of the general through marriage, writes vividly of life with Stuart at his military outposts.

Cooke tells that when he paid a visit to Stuart's "Camp Qui Vive," he felt the old house presented a cold, bare appearance, with horses hitched to trees and soldiers coming and going frequently. By the door was the newly adopted red battle flag. Stuart was devoted to artillery and next to the flag was a Blakely gun. Guarding the gun was an enormous raccoon, with snapping eyes and a ready snarl, which the fun-loving general had placed there as a sentinel.

For all the camp's outward appearance of coldness, its twenty-seven year old commander was the first to call for a song or a dance or a game. Ambitious, jovial, and possessing an enormous physical strength, Stuart was truly a splendid war machine and loved nothing better than to clash with the enemy.

Everything about Stuart's appearance was youthful and picturesque. Though small in stature, he loved the pageantry of dress. While other prominent soldiers of the time seemed to avoid any tendency toward display in their dress, Stuart was the exact opposite, for he loved gay colors. His fighting jacket was brilliant with dazzling buttons and gold braid. His hat was looped up with a golden star and decorated with a black ostrich plume. He tied a yellow sash around his waist and wore buff gauntlets that reached to his elbow. His spurs were of gold and his cloak lined with scarlet.

Many persons scoffed at Stuart, saying he was unfit for his post. They sneered at his costume, his laughter, his love of the ladies, the banjo player who always accompanied him, his flower-wreathed horses and his gay songs. His enemies, however, were not numbered among them. They had felt the man's force too often and knew well his capabilities as a leader and as a soldier.

Stuart's love for little children was apparent everywhere he went. Mr. R. M. Loughborough, former Executive Secretary of Fairfax County, still has in his possession a lock of General Stuart's hair that was given to Mr. Loughborough's mother when she was a little girl. A statement in her handwriting, preserved with the lock of hair, reads as follows:

"A lock of General J. E. B. Stuart's hair, presented to me by himself which I made into this cross. I asked him for a button from his coat and he said, 'My dear little girl, would you not rather have a lock of my hair? If I gave every little girl a button from my coat that wanted one I should have none left on my coat.' "

General Stuart was loved deeply by those who knew him well. His deep devotion to his wife and young children was plain for all to see, for he never seemed so satisfied as when they were with him. When the news reached him of the death of his little daughter Flora, he was almost overcome and said he would never recover from the sorrow her death brought. Yet, he was a remarkable leader -- indomitable despite tremendous strain. In official affairs Stuart appeared to be a hard man and nothing seemed to move him. Yet, he jested with the soldiers and they felt no restraint in his presence. He dearly loved a joke, for he had a keen sense of humor, but there was no sarcasm about him. He jested in a rough fashion and the men who served under him were welcome to return the jest in a like manner. He enjoyed life and lived it to the fullest, but he held strong prejudices and never forgave disobedience. He declined invitations if his staff was not included in them. All in all, he was one of the most beloved generals of the period.

Stuart was an expert rider and the speed at which he rode frequently saved his life. Seemingly, he led a charmed life, for he had never been injured until the fatal day in May 1864 at Yellow Tavern, when the bullet that struck him ended his life. He was thirty-two years of age at the time of his death.

A great deal of the romance and splendor of Virginia's chivalry died with Stuart, who has been called "the flower of the cavaliers."

Fairfax Courthouse

Professor Lowe and His Balloon

Thaddeus S. C. Lowe, distinguished aeronaut, meteorologist, and inventor, played an important role during the Civil War, rendering valuable service to the Army of the Potomac -- from Bull Run to Gettysburg -- with his balloon ascensions.

Professor Lowe first became interested in ballooning as a means of investigating upper air currents. In 1858, he made his initial air voyage from Ottawa, Canada, in connection with the celebration of the laying of the first Atlantic cable.

Lowe claimed he was the first prisoner taken by the Confederates in the Civil War. On April 20, 1861, he left Cincinnati, Ohio, in his balloon and after traveling some nine hundred miles in nine hours, landed near Pea Ridge, close to the boundary between North and South Carolina. Southerners, thinking he was a Yankee spy, arrested him at once, and for a while he was in serious danger of violence from the mob that gathered. Finally, a man who had witnessed an ascent Lowe had made at Charleston, South Carolina, the previous year, identified him and vouched for him as a scientific investigator who was not connected with military matters.

Shortly after that, however, Lowe went to Washington for the purpose of interesting military authorities in his balloon. On June 17, 1861, he made an ascension in Washington with the balloon connected by telegraph to the War Department. To President Lincoln, Lowe sent the first message ever telegraphed from a balloon. It read:

"Balloon Enterprise
"Washington, June 17, 1861

"To the President of the United States

"Sir: This point of observation commands an area nearly fifty miles in diameter. The city and its girdle of encampments, presents a superb scene. I take great pleasure in sending you this first dispatch ever telegraphed from an aerial station and in acknowledging my indebtedness to your encouragement for the opportunity of demonstrating the availability of the science of aeronautics in the military service of the country.

"Yours respectfully,
"T. S. C. Lowe"

Soon Thaddeus Lowe was empowered to organize the Aeronautical Corps of the Army, and he made numerous ascensions with his balloon. It was inflated with hydrogen in Washington and then towed across the river and the ascension made from the Virginia side of the Potomac.

On one occasion, a Major Colburn of the Connecticut Regiment accompanied the professor on an ascension and made a sketch of the country. It was so accurate that Virginians, familiar with the vicinity of Fairfax

Courthouse, recognized lanes, roads, and houses. It was then decided that maps of the entire country occupied by Confederate troops should be made from the air under Lowe's guidance.

The pioneer aeronaut of his time, Lowe was in constant danger and on one occasion narrowly missed disaster when he was fired upon by Confederate troops while he was making an ascension at Ball's Crossroads.

After the war, Lowe became interested in the manufacture of artificial ice and has been credited as being the first in the United States to manufacture ice commercially.

While living in California from 1891 to 1894, Lowe became known for his construction of an inclined railway at Rubio Canyon and Echo Mountain. A peak near the well-known Mt. Wilson was named Mt. Lowe in his honor, and Professor Lowe equipped and maintained an observatory on the summit.

Lowe's last days were spent at Pasadena, California.

Professor Thaddeus S.C. Lowe

Clara Barton, Heroine of the Second Battle of Manassas

Casualties sustained in the Civil War were greater in number than the total American casualties resulting from all other wars in which the United States has been involved -- from the Revolution through the Korean conflict. The shocking total of 618,000 deaths was due in part to the fact that provisions for first aid on the battlefields were inadequate, and to the fact that the Medical Corps was lacking in equipment, medicines, and supplies. Yet, casualties probably would have been even greater, had it not been for Clara H. Barton, who did her utmost to provide care for the wounded soldiers.

Clara Barton's interest in caring for the injured began when she was a small child and her brother David fell from the rafters of a barn, sustaining such serious injuries that for two years he was bedridden. During the period of convalescence, Clara was his nurse and companion and remained with him constantly. This incident probably shaped her role in later life.

The early part of her career was spent in teaching school, but after a few years she decided to give up teaching and went to Washington, D. C., where she worked for a time in the Patent Office. After the outbreak of the Civil War, she learned that many of the boys who had been her pupils were now soldiers, and that some had been wounded in battle and brought to Washington. She saw an opportunity to serve as "mother to an army," and with her own funds bought needed items for the wounded men quartered in the unfinished Senate Chamber of the Capitol. Miss Barton advertised in the newspapers of her home town (Worcester, Massachusetts) for additional supplies. The response was huge donations of medicines, bandages, food, and other articles.

Reports of the steadily increasing number of casualties meant one thing to Miss Barton: an emergency call for service -- not to the Blue or to the Gray, but to all wounded and suffering soldiers. She gathered bandages, dressings, and food from voluntary donors. Then, overriding the regulations of the army and the conventions of society, Miss Barton obtained permission to work close to the battle lines, and authority to send supplies by train from Alexandria to the battlefront. She then drove in her carriage from her home in Washington to the railway yards west of Alexandria, where she entrained for the front. She took along a large supply of candles and cooking utensils, but her personal belongings were so few she was able to carry them tied in a large handkerchief.

At the dedication at Fairfax Station of the commemorative marker honoring Miss Barton, Brigadier General William A. Collier described the battle scene at Manassas when Miss Barton arrived there:

Clara Barton

General Collier's speech continued:

"Miss Barton and her small group immediately set about to stop the bleeding of the injured and to dress and bandage wounds. As the day passed and no military rations became available, this determined woman prepared to feed the hungry. With almost no utensils other than two water buckets, five dippers, and one stew pan, she proceeded to do what the fainthearted would have considered an impossible task. She had brought coffee, hard crackers, jams, jellies and other food and as the jam jars and jelly tumblers were emptied, she filled them again and again with soup or coffee or bread soaked in stimulating wine."

Clara Barton broke open bales of hay for use as mattresses and for protection from the rain. By night the food supplies were almost gone, so she took the leftovers and made a mixture of hard crackers pounded into crumbs, together with wine, brown sugar, and hot water. This she fed to the wounded men. During the night her activities increased. She made compresses and slings and bound wounds. She did everything "from administering her famous gruel to holding dying soldiers in her arms and sought to give each wounded soldier what he most needed, a letter home, a prayer, to ease his pain, appease his hunger or quiet his fears. And those ragged bloody men, who said everything but their prayers, were deeply grateful."

The next day more wounded were brought in, and food supplies had to be replenished. When a few empty railroad trains arrived, Miss Barton organized the loading of the wounded, making sure that each received some nourishment before he was evacuated. During pouring rain and lightning, and the noise of artillery fire from the engagement near Chantilly, she continued her service to the men. She answered countless letters. "While our soldiers can stand and fight," she wrote in her diary, "I can stand and feed and nurse them."

In his speech, General Collier went on to say:

"During this third afternoon, many Federal troops including the remnants of Kearny's division of Heintzelman's III Corps, withdrew through the Fairfax Station area enroute to Alexandria. This plus a Confederate cavalry raid expected momentarily through the woods south of the railroad, from the rapidly closing in left flank, added to the confusion.

"Because the situation looked dim, she sent her volunteer helpers back but she herself remained throughout the evening until the last of more than three thousand wounded had been evacuated. Only then did she leave and then on the last train. Soon thereafter Fairfax Station changed hands."

Although Clara Barton faced grave dangers while serving at Fairfax Station, she worked tirelessly and served with tremendous courage and unselfish dedication. Later the founder of the American Red Cross, Clara Barton has often been described as "the angel of the battlefield." Surely, the title was well deserved.

"It was on a Sunday morning, August 31, 1862, that the main battle reached its peak and the wooded acres immediately north of the little railway depot were filled with hundreds of wounded soldiers. The more critical and serious cases were cared for in and around the picturesque St. Mary's Church which still stands, serene with its wooded background. There the wounded awaited transportation to makeshift hospitals in Alexandria and Washington."
Additional wounded arrived during the remainder of the day. Wounded soldiers lay on the ground among the trees and the entire area was soon filled with wounded and dying men.

Historical Commemorative Marker at Fairfax Station

The Rebel Yell

The Rebel yell was first heard in the First Battle of Manassas and has been described in various ways. One person said that it sounded like "forty thousand wildcats," while another described it as "one long sustained cry on the major third of the male falsetto." Still others remembered that it "began like a low growl and rose to a falsetto scream." Regardless of how it sounded, it became as much a part of the Confederate soldier's fighting equipment as his musket. Most likely, the call served as a release for the soldier's fear, excitement, and taut nerves, as well as a means of scaring the enemy.

The yell varied to some extent with the troops, and the Virginian's yell was somewhat different from that of the Mississipian. Whatever the variation, the Yankees were so impressed that in 1869, four years after the war, according to Roy M. Thompson, a columnist for the Biloxi Daily Herald, the soccer team at Princeton used a blood chilling adaptation of it in a game with Rutgers. It was a Princeton victory, 8 to 0. At first the team did their own yelling, but since this took needed energy and interfered with their play, the onlooking students took over, and thus organized college and high school rooting was born -- a direct outgrowth of the famed Rebel yell.

Fairfax Courthouse, 1862. Note original windows.

Antonia Ford

Antonia Ford of Fairfax

Antonia Ford of Fairfax possessed a deep devotion to the Confederacy, and today her name is remembered along with that of Belle Boyd, another famous woman who served the Confederacy as a spy.

What sort of person was Antonia? She was a strikingly beautiful woman, vibrant with life and energy, capable of making her own decisions, and possessing a native wit. Her art of conversation was to become an important asset as war came to her quiet home in Fairfax.

Shortly after the Civil War began, the country hamlet became a focal point in the plans of both Union and Confederate strategists. And the Ford home developed into a center for social activities for troops from both sides. While Southern soldiers were entertained by preference, Northern men were also made welcome through force of circumstances. Antonia was popular with both and soon began to realize that she might trade on that popularity to help the Confederacy with vital information gleaned from unsuspecting Union soldiers who were captivated by her wit and charm.

Antonia became so successful in her espionage work that Cavalry General J. E. B. Stuart issued a document which read:

"TO WHOM IT MAY CONCERN:

"Know ye: that reposing special confidence in the patriotism, fidelity and ability of Miss Antonia Ford, I, James E. B. Stuart, by virtue of the power vested in me, as Brigadier General in the Provisional Army of the Confederate States of America, do hereby appoint and commission her my honorary aide-de-camp, to rank as such from this date.

"She will be obeyed, respected and admired by all the lovers of a noble nature.

"Given under my hand and seal at the headquarters, Cavalry Brigade, at Camp Beverly, this seventh day of October, A. D., 1861, and the first year of our Independence.

"James E. B. Stuart
"Brigadier General, CSA"

Ironically, it was this document that proved to be Antonia's undoing two years later.

It was on the evening of March 8, 1863, that Colonel John Singleton Mosby captured General Edwin H. Stoughton at Fairfax. The next morning, Union officers ordered all who were thought to have supplied Mosby with information to be rounded up. Evidence pointed to Antonia, for her previous activities and her close association with General Stuart gave the Union officers reason to be suspicious. The Ford home was searched and Antonia's commission from Stuart was found. Both Antonia and her father were immediately placed under arrest.

Ford Building in City of Fairfax, originally the home of Antonia Ford.

Union Major Joseph C. Willard, who had visited the Ford home on many occasions and had fallen under Antonia's spell, came to take her to the old Capital Prison pending further inquiry. Immediately after placing her behind bars, Willard set to work to secure her release. Before many months had passed, he was successful and both Antonia and her father were freed and returned to their home. It appears unlikely that she resumed her espionage activities after that time, for the seven months' imprisonment proved detrimental to Antonia's health, and the once beautiful girl began to lose her vitality and strength.

Joseph Willard had been in love with Antonia for some time, and now he asked her to become his wife. Antonia accepted his proposal and they were married in Washington, D. C., on March 10, 1864. The Willards lived in Washington after their marriage and had three children -- all sons -- but only one, Joseph E. Willard, survived.

Antonia's health had suffered greatly and seven years after her marriage she died and was buried in Oak Hill Cemetery in Washington. Young Joseph was sent to Fairfax to live with the Ford family, but Antonia's father died shortly after she did and the boy was reared by Antonia's sister.

Joseph Willard and his brother Henry continued to run the famous establishment they had founded in Washington -- the Willard Hotel. Although he was a devoted father and spent as much time as possible with his son, Joseph Willard mourned the loss of Antonia for the remainder of his life.

The son was educated in Virginia schools and received a law degree from the University of Virginia. He won distinction in local law practice, was elected lieutenant governor, and later ran for governor but was defeated.

Upon his father's death, young Joseph inherited the hotel. He married a Virginia girl, Belle Wyatt, and they had two daughters, Belle and Elizabeth. Belle married Kermit Roosevelt in 1913, and Elizabeth married a son of the Fifth Earl of Caernarvon, British archaeologist, who, with Howard Carter, discovered the tomb of King Tut-ankh-amen.

Antonia's memory lingers on in the town where once she lived, and one hears and sees the names of Ford and Willard frequently. On June 10, 1951, the Fairfax Chapter of the United Daughters of the Confederacy dedicated a carillon in the Fairfax Methodist Church to the memory of Antonia and her wartime exploits. The Fairfax public library and the Joseph Willard Health Center stand on ground that was formerly part of the Willard estate. Part of the Ford building on Chain Bridge Road, near Main Street in Fairfax, is Antonia's girlhood home.

Towns and Settlements in Fairfax County

ANNANDALE

The community of Annandale had a humble beginning as an Indian village, and later became a trading post where early settlers and Indians bartered for goods. It is believed that the small settlement was named by English immigrants in honor of the Earl of Annandale, Robert de Brus, a thirteenth century knight of the Northern Border who later became a King of Scotland.

Among Annandale's first businesses was the small tollhouse established late in the eighteenth century on the Little River Turnpike. The tollhouse, built crudely of logs, was later covered with clapboard and painted white. Although the building is no longer standing, it is interesting to note that it served as the voting place for the precinct when it came time for Virginians in the area to decide whether they wanted to remain in the Union or join the Confederacy. Thirty-three votes were cast: twenty-nine for secession and four against it.

The Annandale area is rich in Civil War history and legend. Twice the remnants of the Army of the Potomac retreated through the community after defeats at Manassas; and Mosby played havoc around the area, raiding Federal communications and supply trains in the vicinity of Annandale.

Return of a Federal Foraging Party to camp near Annandale.

Bailey's Crossroads

Bailey's Crossroads has long been an important center in Fairfax County. From the time the Northern Neck was first settled, the Crossroads marked the junction of early "rolling roads" on which were transported the hogsheads of tobacco brought from the Shenandoah Valley to Alexandria. Later, Bailey's Crossroads became a trading center with a hotel-boarding house, tavern, mill, and a few stores to serve the needs of the nearby dairy farmers.

In 1763, when Colonel George Washington led troops to the relief of Fort Defiance, they stopped overnight on the great plateau extending from the present site of the Washington-Virginia Airport to Munson's Hill.

During the early part of the Civil War, Abraham Lincoln reviewed 70,000 Union troops encamped on the same plain. He was accompanied by numerous Cabinet members and Government officials, as well as many Washington residents who rode out in carriages to witness the ceremony. One of those in the audience was Julia Ward Howe. Both during and after the review, she heard the song "John Brown's Body" sung frequently. While she liked the melody, she did not like the lyrics. So, back in her hotel room at the Willard House, she wrote the verses that later became famous as "The Battle Hymn of the Republic." Thus, Bailey's Crossroads has gone down in history as having played an important part in the inspiration that led to the composition of one of the most widely sung hymns in the history of the Nation.

Street scene, Centreville.

Centreville

The town of Centreville, which began as a village called "Newgate," was undoubtedly the first town or village established in what is now Fairfax County, for Newgate came into being sometime before 1730. King Carter and his friends had patented great tracts in the area, assuming the land would be suitable for the cultivation of tobacco, but the planting of tobacco and other crops brought only indifferent success. So by 1760, when land speculation subsided, the forest had once again reclaimed many of the fields, and the village of Newgate was marked only by the continued existence of a church, a grist mill, and a store.

In 1791 merchants in Alexandria proposed construction of a turnpike to run from Alexandria to the Rappahannock below the present town of Warrenton. Acting on the assumption that the turnpike would follow the then-existing road through Newgate, landholders near the village proposed establishment of a new town. On November 12, 1792, the Virginia Assembly approved the charter for the town, which was to be named Centreville. Building of the turnpike was delayed and in the meantime the Little River Turnpike from Alexandria to Aldie was completed, so freight from the Shenandoah, which previously had used the road through Newgate, now took the new, direct route. Then plans for the turnpike to the Rappahannock were abandoned and the town of Centreville lapsed once again into obscurity.

Land speculation in the Centreville area was once more renewed in 1853 by the proposal that a section of the Manassas Gap Railroad be built in the vicinity. However, the War Between the States put a stop to the construction before it could bring the expected impetus to the town. Nevertheless, the war made the town famous, for the Battle of Bull Run brought Centreville to the attention of the entire nation, and for four years it was much in the news as an armed camp alternately occupied by Union and Confederate forces.

Although it has never become important industrially, Centreville, during the past hundred years, has become increasingly important to historians and tourists as a center of historical interest.

Hotel at Clifton

CLIFTON

The small, quiet town of Clifton, in southwest Fairfax County, was once one of the county's most prominent communities. A popular resort town during the post-Civil War years, it was the home of Paradise Springs, and people came from miles away to bathe in the health-giving waters and to drink of the healing elixir.

The earliest known commercial activity in the vicinity of Clifton was the old soapstone mine which is also said to have been a source of soapstone for the Indians in pre-Colonial days. Evidence supporting the belief lies in the fact that even today, many arrowheads are to be found in the forests and along the streams in the area.

Clifton was incorporated as a town in 1902 but has grown slowly through the years. Serious consideration has been given to plans for the restoration of the town, incorporating the residents' desire to preserve the charm of the elegant old Victorian structures, yet providing up-to-date transportation, as well as modern housing, shopping, and recreational facilities. Among the landmarks cited for restoration is the old Clifton Hotel, which at various times was frequented by Ulysses S. Grant, Colonel John S. Mosby, and President Chester Arthur.

FAIRFAX

The county seat of Fairfax County was moved from Alexandria to its present location in 1799, and construction of the courthouse building was completed in 1800. Gradually, a village grew up around the new courthouse, and in 1805, the settlement was established officially as the town of Providence, with the Providence District deriving its name from the settlement. Originally, Culpeper was known by the name "Fairfax," but in 1859 Culpeper abandoned the name by which it had been known since 1759 and assumed the name of its county. Once Culpeper officially abandoned the name "Fairfax," Fairfax County appropriated the name for its county seat. In 1874, by Act of the General Assembly, the county seat was incorporated as the town of Fairfax. Then, in March 1961, the county seat once more changed its status, becoming the City of Fairfax.

Built in the early eighteenth century, the Blincoe House, formerly located on Main Street just east of Earp's Ordinary, was probably the oldest house in the town of Fairfax.

Schoolhouse at Clifton

FLORIS — FRYING PAN

Floris, a community two miles west of Herndon, has for generations been the center of a prosperous farming area, from which the railroad picked up the dairyman's milk and took it to the city, and to which, in turn, the railroad brought the farmer his supplies. Among the buildings of historical significance is the old Frying Pan Baptist Church, which pre-dates the Civil War, and which was built to replace an older structure on the same site that was partly destroyed during the Revolution.

FRANCONIA

Franconia is another community that was established as the result of the farmers' need for a local trading center. Although the area was not of great commercial significance, the community became an important stop on the rail line between Washington and Quantico, and shortly after the Civil War, a railraod station was built there. According to the custom of the time, anyone granting a right of way to a railroad had the privilege of naming the station built on his property. Thus, Franconia Station was named after the Franconia Farm.

Historic stone bridge across Bull Run.

Eldon Street, Herndon

HERNDON

In 1856-57, the new railroad from Alexandria was completed as far as the site of the present town of Herndon, and a turn-around table was constructed where the town hall now stands. Residents of the area, foreseeing the possibility of commercial development, decided it would be beneficial to have their own post office. Before the post office could be established, however, postal authorities required that the area be named. Consequently, a meeting of the local citizens was called, and the question of a name for the area was discussed. Eventually, approval was given the suggestion that the community be named "Herndon" in memory of William Lewis Herndon, a brave American sea captain who, shortly before that, had gone down with his ship in a storm, after first making sure that all others aboard were safely transferred to lifeboats. With the name approved, the post office was opened on July 13, 1858.

In 1879, Herndon was incorporated with an area of four and one-third square miles of land inside its borders. The town site is said to have been made this large so that saloons could not be established within easy walking distance of the railroad station and so create a "town nuisance."

The railroad provided ready access for the city families who wanted to vacation in the country, and a number of spacious summer houses were built in Herndon by Washington families.

The town charter, which was modernized in 1938, provides for the election every two years of a mayor and six councilmen, while other officials are appointed.

1910 photo of Herndon

Langley, Lewinsville and McLean

Langley and Lewinsville were about three miles apart on what is now Route 123. The two were villages complete in themselves, each with its own post office, although there was no definite dividing line between the two. Langley took its name from the Langley Mansion of the Lee family, while Lewinsville was named for one of the families that first settled in the area.

For many years the Langley Hotel was a stopping place for stagecoaches running from Leesburg and points west to Georgetown. During the War Between the States, the hotel as well as the Salona, Rokeby, and Langley Mansions served as headquarters for various Union officers in charge of nearby army outposts.

Following the war, Langley and Lewinsville remained quiet little villages until about 1909 when the Elkins Estate of West Virginia and John R. McLean, owner and publisher of the "Washington Post," decided to establish an electric car line from Rosslyn to Cumberland, Maryland, and routed a spur line to Great Falls via the area between Langley and Lewinsville. At the point where the "Great Falls and Old Dominion Railroad" crossed the road between the two villages, the passenger and freight station was erected. Originally the station bore the name of "Ingleside," but later the name was changed to "McLean," after John R. McLean.

The advent of the railroad brought many changes. The voting place, which had been at Langley, was moved to McLean and became known as "Langley Precinct." Then the post offices at Langley and Lewinsville were abolished and a central post office was set up at McLean.

Old Dominion Drive (which derived its name from the railroad) follows the old road bed of the now defunct electric car line.

Colvin Run Mill, near Route 7, was once owned by George Washington

Toll Gate on Route 123 at Oakton

OAKTON

Oakton, on Route 123 about halfway between Fairfax and Vienna, was known in earlier days as Flint Hill. But in 1880 when Mr. Squire E. Smith filed application for a post office for the community, the name "Flint Hill" was rejected, for there was already a post office by that name in Rappahannock County. Mr. Smith decided the name "Oakton" would be appropriate, since the huge oak tree in the intersection of highways 123 and 674 (Hunter's Mill Road) had long been a landmark of the community.

The one-room Flint Hill School, said to have first been in session in 1849-50, is believed by many historians to have been the first public school in Fairfax County. The building burned shortly after the Civil War and was replaced by a second one-room school at the same intersection. Through the years, the buildings housing the Oakton School have been enlarged and eventually replaced several times, but current facilities are still at the same location.

Oakton school building number one as it appeared in 1875, showing tree for which Oakton was named.

Springfield

About 1854, after the Orange and Alexandria Railroad was completed, the name Springfield was given to the railroad station built at the Backlick Road crossing. Until Shirley Highway was completed, Springfield was only a whistle stop on the railroad line, and residents of the community lived on farms or in country homes. Although the railroad played an important part in the lives of residents of the area prior to the turn of the century, the tremendous increase in the population of Springfield is attributed largely to the super-highway which brings Washington within easy commuting distance.

Vienna

Vienna is another of the many Fairfax County communities with roots deep in the past. Originally it was called "Ayr Hill," the name given it by a Scotch immigrant in memory of his former home. Later, when a man by the name of Hendricks was looking for a community in which to settle, local citizens agreed to change the name, for they felt his enterprises could bring economic impetus to the town and were anxious to please him. So the name "Ayr Hill" was changed to "Vienna," which was the name of Hendricks' former home in New York State.

The first house had been built in the community in 1767, but Vienna did not become an incorporated town until 1890. Covering an area of 4.29 square miles, Vienna is approximately in the center of Fairfax County. It has a Council-Manager form of government and maintains departments of Public Works, Police, Finance, Planning, and Recreation. It also has its own volunteer fire department, although the school system and health and welfare programs are provided by Fairfax County. Predominately a residential community of single family homes, the town has made provisions for a balanced community with limited apartments, and commercial and light industrial areas.

Maple Avenue, Vienna

Wiehle — now Reston

In 1833, Thomas Fairfax and his wife, Margaret, deeded to three of their sons various parcels of land totalling thirteen thousand acres. In 1843, they deeded to a fourth son, Reginald, a parcel of 8,035 acres (including what is now the Reston project) and another parcel of 481 acres. Reginald was in the United States Navy in the Cape Verde Islands, so in 1851 he appointed Joshua C. Gunnell to execute a deed for these lands to a Benjamin Thornton of Orange County.

Near the railroad station at what became known as Thornton Station, or Thornton's Mills, Benjamin Thornton built a home in the gothic style, which stood until 1955 when it was destroyed by fire.

The area was the scene of some action during the Civil War. On September 3, 1862, General Lee and his men marched up the old Ox Road and along the Ridge Road (now Route 602), through what is now Reston, on their way to Antietam.

After the war, Virginia was a favorite area for speculators, and rumors spread that the area was rich in minerals. A mineral fever followed and geologists and cartographers were employed to locate the riches in the soil. Many Northerners came to the area and it became fashionable for Washington's wealthy to buy Virginia land, build mansions, and make of themselves Virginia gentry.

One such wealthy citizen was Dr. Carl Adolf Max Wiehle. The doctor, son of a minister of the German Reformed Church, had gone to Philadelphia as a small boy. He was educated at the University of Pennsylvania and practiced medicine in Philadelphia. He married and had seven children. Dr. Wiehle prospered and at the age of thirty-five retired with a comfortable fortune. Then in 1881 he moved to Washington and built a home at 1621 Connecticut Avenue.

The Doctor joined with William Dunn, one of the founders of Dunn Loring, to purchase a large tract of land. The two paid $20,000 for land that was being sold to satisfy claims against its owner. The tract was divided so that Dunn and his wife had 3,221 acres, and Dr. Wiehle and his wife, 3,228 acres. Dunn's land lay south of the railroad tracks, while most of Dr. Wiehle's land lay to the north. During the next several years, Dr. Wiehle purchased other tracts to increase his holdings.

At Thornton's Mills, Dr. Wiehle built a summer home of gingerbread architecture, overlooking the handsome property he constantly improved. There were three hand-dug lakes, and a wooden bridge spanning the middle one. A thirty foot square ice house was built on the property, and the ice cutting was an event to which the whole family came from Washington. It is interesting to note that this building housed the first offices of the distillery built on the property in 1935, and today contains offices of the Internal Revenue men assigned to the distillery.

Dr. Wiehle dreamed of building a model city on his land and worked continually toward that goal. He renamed the area "Wiehle" and a post office by that name was located on the property on August 22, 1887. He brought from Germany a city planner to lay out his town. The streets were named Paris, London, Berlin, and Vienna -- reflecting his European heritage. Other streets were named for his children and still others were named for various trees.

The first industry located at Wiehle was the Maryland and Virginia Serpentine and Talc Company of Baltimore. Talc and soapstone were mined on the land, and a brick kiln and sawmill provided the building materials for the first structures in the town.

A. Smith Bowman, Jr., in his History of Sunset Hills Farm, writes of one of the town's first structures, the Aesculapian Hotel:

"This was a rambling thirty-five room building with towers, gables and many porches. It sported a bowling alley and tennis courts, the lakes afforded swimming, fishing and boating and the surrounding woods offered cool bridle paths and good hunting. This was appropriately named the Aesculapian Hotel by its physician builder and was filled to capacity each summer at monthly rates of $30.00 including board. Its chef had once worked for J. P. Morgan and its cuisine and the excellent quality of its spring water was known for miles around. There was a continual waiting list."

Dr. Wiehle did not live long enough to see his dream town materialize, for in 1901, he died in Washington of pneumonia. The newspapers reported that one of Washington's richest German-Americans had passed away. His friends, however, said the doctor's dream town had failed and that his finances were at rock bottom.

The property changed hands many times after the death of Dr. Wiehle and finally in 1927, A. Smith Bowman bought four thousand acres on the north side of the tracks as well as the Wiehle home. In 1934, after the repeal of Prohibition, Mr. Bowman built the famous distillery that makes "Virginia Gentleman" and "Fairfax County" bourbon whiskies. The name "Wiehle" was eventually dropped and the post office officially changed to "Sunset Hills."

In 1947 the Bowmans bought the Dunn tract south of the railroad, bringing the acreage of Sunset Hills Farm to about 7,200 acres and making it the largest farm in Northern Virginia. A landmark in the area, the farm became the home of the famous Fairfax Hunt. During the 1930's, Dr. Wiehle's hotel was used for hunt breakfasts and balls, but the building was torn down in 1956 after it was damaged by fire.

The farm and distillery were sold in 1960 to Lefcourt Realty Corporation. The corporation in turn sold the farm but not the distillery to Palindrome Corporation, headed by Robert E. Simon, Jr., who is presently developing the land, under the name of "Reston," into one of the country's newest type cities.

Aesculapian Hotel, Wiehle

OTHER VILLAGES AND COMMUNITIES

Thornton, Taylors, Mt. Olive Chapel, Arlington Mills Station, Mill's Crossroads, Great Falls, Germantown, Daingerfield, Sangster Station, Fort Buffalo, and Brimstone Hill are names of other villages and communities included on maps of Northern Virginia a century ago. With the continued urbanization of Fairfax County, the many small communities have either merged geographically with larger communities and towns or have lost their original identity through a complete change of name. Thus, Fairfax County has lost much local color formerly provided by the distinctive and often intriguing community names fittingly applied in colonial and ante bellum days. And, unfortunately, most of the changes in terminology have left today's county residents euphoniously the poorer.

Historic Facts

"Belhaven," located at the southern edge of the present City of Alexandria, was the first permanent English settlement in the area that later became Fairfax County.

Captain Robert Howson and a band of about 120 men were the first English settlers in Fairfax County. They established Belhaven on the grant of 6,600 acres made to Captain Howson by Governor Berkeley of Virginia in 1669.

Fairfax County was created in 1742.

Freedom Hill, near the present site of Tyson's Corner, was the first county seat and was established in 1743.

The original house on the Mt. Vernon Estate was built by Lawrence Washington in 1743.

Gunston Hall, the home of George Mason, was built in 1757-58.

The "Fairfax Independent Company of Volunteers," the first organized militia in the Colonies, came into being through a plan evolved by George Mason, one of Fairfax County's most illustrious citizens, and the first Captain of the Militia was George Washington.

George Johnson, a distinguished lawyer of Fairfax, was the author of the resolutions introduced in the House of Burgesses by Patrick Henry denouncing the Stamp Act. Johnson wrote the resolutions on the fly leaf of a law book and they were offered by Henry (who it is claimed was erroneously credited with their authorship), supported in an able speech by Johnson.

The first meeting that threatened armed resistance to Great Britain was held in Fairfax County and was presided over by George Washington. It declared in its resolutions, "If Boston submits, we will not."

The "Fairfax Resolves," first clearly written statement defining the Colonies' rights in relation to England, were authored by George Mason. Adopted by the Virginia Legislature in August 1774, they became known as the "Virginia Resolves" and later were adopted by the Continental Congress.

The "Virginia Declaration of Rights," drawn up by George Mason, became the basis for the Declaration of Independence drafted in 1776 by Thomas Jefferson.

The Virginia Constitution, the first "written constitution of a free commonwealth," was also written by George Mason.

Despite the fact that many of his ideas were incorporated into the Constitution of the United States, George Mason refused to sign the Constitution and openly campaigned against its ratification in Virginia because he opposed a central government with unfixed powers. As a result of his efforts, the "subsequent Amendments," which he wrote, were introduced in Congress and adopted as the "Bill of Rights."

George Washington, Fairfax County's most eminent citizen of all time, became the leader of Colonial forces in the War for Independence, and later became the first President of the United States.

The town of Providence (now the City of Fairfax) was created in 1805.

One of the first telegraph lines in the world ran through Fairfax County. Built by the Washington-New Orleans Telegraph Company in 1847, the line ran from Washington to Petersburg, Virginia.

James W. Jackson, the first Southern man killed in the Civil War, was killed in Alexandria on May 24, 1861.

Captain John Q. Marr, the first Southern man "killed in battle," was killed at Fairfax Courthouse on June 1, 1861.

The first battle of any magnitude in the Civil War was fought on Fairfax soil on July 18, 1861 and is known as the Battle of Bull Run.

The last fight of the Civil War on Virginia soil was at Arundels, Fairfax County, and was fought on April 10, 1865, between two companies of Mosby's men (under Captain Baylor) and a detachment of the Eighth Illinois Cavalry (under Captain Warner).

Episcopal High School, one of the oldest preparatory schools for boys in the South, was founded in Fairfax County in 1839.

The first public school in the county is believed to have been located at Oakton in 1849.

Masonic Hall, Fairfax

Fairfax County Today

Fairfax County is currently adding fifteen hundred persons per month to a population that totaled 316,210 in mid-1964. It is anticipated that by the year 2000, the county's population will exceed one million people. The county is presently attempting to take the local government out into the field, so to speak, in order to serve the residents of the vast area more adequately. At satellite information centers, assistance with income tax forms and information regarding the county may be obtained, as well as auto tags and dog licenses.

The county today boasts effective transportation facilities, an adequate water supply, and a "Master Plan" that serves as a general guide to insure its citizens of efficient and orderly growth in all areas. One of the largest singly owned school bus fleets in the world belongs to Fairfax County.

Since 1959, a growing circulation has kept Fairfax County Public Libraries the largest system in the Commonwealth, in volume of business. Services offered include bookmobiles, films, excellent research facilities, records, a talking book service for shut-ins, and at the headquarters library in Fairfax, a listening station where eight persons may listen simultaneously to one recording.

The county boasts one of the most highly educated populaces in the Nation, as the result of the military, governmental, and scientific concentration in the area. Its citizens therefore place high demands on education, governing bodies, and public services, and are constantly working to attain their goals.

The last decade in Fairfax County has brought tremendous changes to the once rural area -- economically, industrially, and numerically. As the county moves forward progressively, it combines the rich heritage of the past with the bright promise of the future. The result is that Fairfax County is rapidly becoming one of the Nation's most outstanding urban areas.

Farr's Mill in Fairfax County